For Patsy Kessinger Calloway

An Arson, A Wig, and A Murder

By: Tina M. Cummins

I'd like to dedicate my first novel to Patsy Calloway who is looking down on us from heaven. Patsy, I hope you think this book captures what needed to be said. Wherever you are up there, I hope you're smiling.

Secondly, I'd also like to dedicate this book to Patsy's brother, Darrell Kessinger. On many occasions, Darrell traversed the odds to work to find justice for Patsy. At every turn, he was told that justice would never come. That didn't stop him. Because of his love for his sister, he relentlessly pushed to get answers for the truth in her case, which still continues today. He never gave up on Patsy and has inspired so many others, to have and keep that same mind set. A brother's love for his sister knows few boundaries. Thank you for pursuing justice for Patsy, and for other missing victims. You've turned tragedy into triumph.

To my friends and family that have stuck by me through all of these ordeals, thank you for being there. Thank you for your words of love and encouragement. I'm blessed to have you in my life.

To those law enforcement officials and volunteers who deal with these crises every day, GOD bless you in your endeavors. Thank you for your time and service. I pray your efforts are fruitful and satisfying. I pray that the Lord keeps you safe and guides you along the path of justice.

I would like to include in this dedication, all of the missing victims in the world and their families. To these victims and their families, we're looking, so "**Never give up**." Keep spreading awareness and know that you are in our thoughts and prayers. May God give you answers, in Jesus name, I pray. Amen

Photo courtesy of Darrell Kessinger

Photo courtesy of Darrell Kessinger

Chapters:

Chapter One: In Pursuit of Truth

How does it feel for a family when someone goes missing? That's a question I can't answer because by the grace of GOD, I can only imagine it. I know how I love my family. The mere thought of something bad happening to any one of them sends me to a place where hell is alive and real here on earth. As a woman and caregiver it's my nature to love, but that particular movie playing in my head is so terrifying, I push it out of my mind almost instantly. What if the nightmare doesn't go away? What if the worst happens? These are important questions to ask ourselves if we're ever going to be useful to those going through it.

In September 2010, the daughter of a friend of mine went missing. I went to a vigil for a missing 17-year-old, and I saw her mother. The raw intensity of the pain in her very core was evident in everything about her. She was walking through that living hell, not something we dream about, but something that is alive and ever present. Her heart was hurt so badly, that her physical body was racked with intense pain. As a former nurse, I'm used to asking that question, "On a scale of 1 – 10, what would you rate your pain?" They can't make an accurate scale for mothers who are missing a child. They are present in the universe like a meteor hurling at 100,000 mph, gathering everything in her way to reach her final destination of knowledge and reality. They take every piece of information they get and seek out what was once the center of their own universe, their child, and the wholeness of their life. This love can sometimes apply to a father, sister, brother or anyone who loves so intensely, but especially a mother.

Wanting to help her, I started going on searches almost daily with my friend Larry. I met with people and learned a lot about missing persons' cases. I wanted to help and I wanted to know what happened to her daughter. Not only did I want to stop that pain in that mother's life, but rescue her child if I could. Who am I? I'm nobody special. Rescue someone, me? I'm crippled and not the best candidate as a search and rescue worker, but I knew there had to be some way I could help. That's where my quest began with missing persons. Within a couple of months, I found myself immersed in a very sad world of many families who've had or have someone missing.

In missing person's cases there are many different types of people involved. There are the rubbernecks who only want to see the train wreck. They care briefly or pretend to care so they can get an up close view of the suffering. There are the paid employees, some who have a deep empathy and take their job above and beyond what they ever thought they could do. This sometimes includes those paid employees who pretend to care but put no real effort into finding truth. They put on a good face for the public, but many are self-serving in their involvement. I've seen the social media trolls come out of the woodwork who can be so utterly cruel to the victims and their families. I've seen the heroes, who devote their time; energy; and money; to finding the missing at all or any cost. Many people jump right in to help out of the sheer goodness within their own hearts. When someone is missing, family members don't care about the motivation behind these people, because they want all the help they can get. You never know what tip someone can provide. Having a loved one missing and not knowing what happened to them, has got to be one of the most horrific things a human could go through.

I received a call from my friend, Shellee Hale, about a 19-year-old missing person's case. Shellee Hale has been involved in search and rescue/recovery for twenty-five years. She has several websites on the internet that assist with missing persons' cases. At one time, she also had a radio show based out of Seattle. When this 17-year-old girl went missing, this is how Shellee and I met. We became fast friends and started working on cases together.

This time when she called me, Shellee said that she'd like me to follow up on this particular case for our website MissingPersonsNews.com. She gets hundreds of calls a week for her work, so she has to filter through them. She asked me to call the gentleman who had contacted her about his missing sister. She told me that he'd made several attempts to call her. She said he'd sent her emails and after finally getting through to her, she listened to his story. Shellee thought I could help him. She also runs Psychiccrimefighter.com, which is a private site for psychics and law enforcement to work together cooperatively. I am an administrator on that site and I work as a volunteer journalist for the online news.

From my perspective, Patsy's story begins there. I've worked many cases as a remote viewer for law enforcement, so I wasn't certain if this man wanted me to do a reading for his sister's case, or if he wanted me to write an article for the online news. Turns out it was both. Shellee gave Darrell Kessinger my phone number and so he contacted me. I explained to him what it is that I do and he asked me to do a reading for his sister.

For those of you not familiar with remote viewing, I'll explain. When I'm asked about a specific person or shown a picture, sometimes I pick up on things relating to that person. Energy transfers somehow, and I get pictures or images in my mind of what occurred with that person, and how their disappearance took place. That's the best way I can explain it because I don't understand it fully myself. Another name for remote viewing is Psyops or psychic intuitive. Once I get the images in my mind, I can often do sketches of perpetrators. Sometimes I hear names and can see what happened during the commission of a crime. Sometimes, I can hear answers to questions in my head; in my own voice; that I ask. Things are revealed to me. Information comes in bits and pieces. It is important to get everything documented on paper, or on the site, and time dated. Then, we can see where the pieces fall into place. Some people refer to this as psychic ability, but I don't like to use that term. I prefer the term remote viewer or intuitive, because that's what I do. Some law enforcement officers get "hunches" about a case. They use what they get in their mind in the same way, almost like déjà vu, but without the visual flashes.

Once I explained to him how this works, I told Darrell that I wanted no information about his sister's case. It is imperative that I do raw readings, so the information that comes from those readings is pure. If someone gives me information, I get front-loaded, meaning. the front of my brain is loaded down with things that interfere with the accuracy of my reading. If I'm on the signal, it's usually apparent immediately. If I'm not on the signal, that also becomes evident. Sometimes information isn't confirmed in the onset, but often at a much later time, so it is extremely important to write everything down. That's what happened in Patsy's case.

Before I proceeded, I wanted to know more about Darrell, so we spent a few minutes getting acquainted on the phone. Darrell told me that he was retired from the U.S. Army. He is a search and rescue volunteer with the Jodi Powers Search and Rescue Technologies team. He said he became a volunteer long after the disappearance of his sister and had worked on missing persons cases himself. He told me he was the younger brother of his sister and he has seven children. He hails from Arkansas, but he grew up in Kentucky. Darrell told me that quit does not abide in him. He said he made two promises to his sister. The first was to find justice, and the second to bring her home.

After Darrell had explained a bit about himself, it was my turn. First and foremost, I am a gnostic Christian, Roman Catholic to be precise. I'm a firm believer in GOD Almighty and this is where I believe my information comes from. I explained to Darrell that sometimes I get very graphic images and details of what occurs to a person and who committed the crimes. As a reader, you can believe this or chose not to, it is what it is. I told Darrell, "I've never charged for a reading for a missing or murdered victim's case in my life." As a matter of fact, I've never charged for a reading of any kind, nor do I intend to. I don't do the kind of readings where people ask about money or their love life. I work strictly on missing persons' cases. That said, I understand why some people accept money, but I have no intention of ever doing that, because I feel for me personally, it is an abuse of the gift I was given.

I don't feel it is right to take advantage of anyone, let alone those who've suffered such a tremendous loss, and who are seeking answers about a loved one. It's not about money for me. It's about seeking and finding answers for families of the missing. And so the reading began. For me, it is imperative to seek God first, and then everything else will fall into place if it's his will.

Chapter Two: The Reading

Normally when I read a case, I'm in a very dark, uninterrupted space, without distractions. I like to be face to face with the people I work with, so I ask them to get on Skype with me, so I can work with them one to one. He already had a Skype account so he agreed. On Monday, September 17th, 2012 at 12:08 a.m., Darrell Kessinger and I met on Skype, and I asked him if he was ready for the reading. Darrell wasn't busy and my husband was sleeping, so we agreed to proceed.

I asked Darrell his sister's name and he told me it was Patsy Calloway. When I closed my eyes, I got an image of a gravel driveway going up to a trailer that was tan and white. The trailer sat horizontally in front of me that had three or four steps leading up to it. Behind me, there were trees at the entrance to the long driveway and one tree directly behind me. I could see a black truck with what briefly looked like a camper top and a small two-door, white car, with two people inside the car. I explained to Darrell that I didn't know if this was past, present, or future. When entering the trailer in my mind, the kitchen was on my right. There was a green old carpet in the living room that I could see and a bar or counter off to my right. There was linoleum floor in the kitchen. The living room was on my left. To my far left, there was a hallway that led down to a couple bedrooms and a bathroom. There was a back door across and down the hall from the bathroom.

What happened next terrified me and had me sleeping with one eye open for weeks. I saw a man in that trailer. He was fighting with a woman. He had his arm around her head and was fighting with her in a battle for her life. I could see that he was tall in stature. The woman was short and thin, with short dark brown or black hair. The man who was fighting with the woman was trying to cut her throat and he dragged her down the hall into the bathroom. Before telling Darrell what my mind was showing me, I explained to Darrell that what I was seeing was very graphic. I wanted to throw up. He told me he could handle hearing it and he wanted to know what I was seeing. He asked me to tell him, so I did.

Without giving me any confirmations, Darrell asked me to continue about the people and what they looked like. I told him the man had longer brown hair, just above the shoulders, and a scruffy beard. He was about 6' tall and a very stocky build. He asked me about the people inside the car. I told Darrell, I see a woman and a man is driving. The woman has red hair, and the other man is smaller than the first. He's got brown hair and a mustache, but no beard. I told Darrell that I could sketch out the people I was seeing in my mind onto a computer program, but that it would take about an hour or so for me to send him the images. He agreed that I send him my sketches via email.

Darrell asked me if I got a name or anything in particular about the perpetrators. I didn't get any names but, I did not feel like it was her husband that killed her. For her husband, I get that he is a pedophile or sexual predator. For the brother, I get him as a serial killer. I didn't feel like this was his first time at the circus, rather something he's done before and has done again. I get him in my mind as a sexual deviant, predator, and murderer. For the brother and woman with red hair, the first thing I got immediately in my mind, was the Hooker case, kidnapping of Colleen Stan, except I was calling it the "Holmes" case because I couldn't remember the name.

Darrell asked me about the woman in the car. All I could see of her is that she had red hair and she appeared to me, wearing nursing scrubs. I couldn't see her face. Then the scene changed to a house on fire. Darrell asked me again about the vehicles. What I saw was a black truck parked in front with some sort of camper top, and a white two-door vehicle, parked on the right of the gravel driveway; on the left side of a large tree; with two people sitting inside. The highway was off to my left in the far distance. The scene changed and I saw visuals of carpet or carpet padding, rolled up and stuffed in trash cans. Darrell asked me what they did with his sister and if I could find her remains. I explained to him that I'm not the best at locating remains, but in my mind, I'm being pulled to Southwest from this trailer location. I was also being pulled Southeast near an airport, for human remains. I told him to contact Shellee, because she is better at getting location than I am. I told Darrell that I believed there was a witness, another man that would come forward eventually. I told him that we could work on google maps together and I could try to pinpoint a location. He agreed we could do that at a later time.

Once the reading was finished, Darrell explained to me that he had a pretty good idea of what had happened to his sister. He explained that rumors floated around town for years about her ex-husband and ex-brother-in-law. He told me that Patsy's ex-husband had paid his brother $1,000 to burn down her house so he could collect insurance money. He said the arson took place in August, almost two years before Patsy went missing. Darrell told me he was conflicted and he didn't know which of the brothers or if both were responsible for the disappearance of his sister. I was clearly getting that the brother killed Patsy and not her husband which I relayed to Darrell from the very beginning.

Darrell asked me to write a story for MissingPersonsNews.com to spread the word about Patsy. We agreed that it was a good idea, to see if someone would divulge any new information. I asked Darrell to get me all of the pertinent information that he gathered over the years and I would sit down and write the article. He didn't send me much except photos, but he helped me via Skype with a timeline of events. I knew it was going to take time, because there were many people that needed to be interviewed. Darrell and I agreed that I would do the computer sketches first and I'd send them to him, so he could determine if they were the people Darrell suspected were responsible for Patsy's disappearance. With that, we hung up on Skype and I got to work.

Before I hung up with Darrell, I told him to not discount or confirm anything I told him, and don't give me any details until I finish with my raw readings. After I hung up with Darrell, I started going over what I felt in my head for Patsy's disappearance, and I wrote it all down. Then I started gathering my source information and making a "to do" list for Patsy's case.

The article would take a while, so I had to get in touch with Shellee and let her know what was going on and that I'd need some time away from the websites.

A couple days later, Darrell called me and wanted to get on Skype and wanted to go over a location for Patsy's remains. I went on Google maps and found Hartford, KY. Now I can't remember precisely what I said to Darrell, but I found SR1414 and lead Darrell on a map journey through Hartford, up 231 until I reached SR1414. Darrell said for a bit, I was focused on the area we now know to be Andy Anderson's farm, but then I got side-tracked and focused on an area down near the airport. Later, Darrell found out that a man's body was recovered near the area I pinpointed at the airport. That's unusual for me, because I'm not good with locations. The closest I've ever come was within two blocks, whereas Shellee has been right on the money, on more than one occasion.

Anyway, I had a clear image in my mind of where Patsy was buried and it was in an area I believe could be washed out by a fast-flowing, flooded, river or creek. I could see a shallow grave about 3'X6' and about 4' deep. I could see Patsy lying in the gravesite in my mind. She was wearing her scrubs, and her purse and coat were in there with her. I told Darrell what I was seeing, but I was getting worn out and I would have to pursue it at another time.

Over the next week or so, I continued to work on the article for MissingPersonsNews. I was going back and forth doing some fact checking, printing out emails, etc… Finally I got around to finishing the sketches. I got onto Flashface, a computer program that allows you to make sketches using different facial features. I called Darrell and asked him to contact me on Skype when he could. In the mean time I messed up the 2nd sketch and had to do it over.

Darrell finally called me back on Skype. He was going back and forth between his home in Arkansas and Kentucky and Tennessee. He was doing search and rescue work while trying to keep up with Patsy's case. Anyway, I showed him the first sketch to see whether or not he knew the guy and if it was one of the men he suspected.

He said it looked like Larry Calloway and he asked me if I was sure. I asked him if the man was related to her, but not her husband. He said that Larry was Patsy's husband. I said, "Who is the brother?" "Can you tell me what he looks like?" He said he can't remember exactly what Gene looked like back then. I told him, that's who I believe killed her. I explained to him that the sketches I do aren't exact, because I have to select from a small variety of facial features that exist in the program I use. Also, trying to get down these visual flashes in my mind is like trying to catch and freeze a thought and picture. In my mind, the man in the trailer who was killing Patsy, had his back to me. After showing Darrell the first sketch on Skype, I got to work on the 2nd sketch.

This is my 1st computer sketch for
Comparison for Patsy Calloway
The photo next to the sketch I did was provided by Tanya Cotrell
On September 1st, 2014. Until a few days ago, I hadn't seen a
picture of Larry in his younger years.

On September 26th, 2012 I sent Darrell this message on Skype "I drew a sketch of the man I see in my head in vehicle behind me. The sketch is on Psychiccrimefighter.com in your sister's forum. Please understand that it was 19 years ago, and I'm using flashface to do the sketch."

[9/26/2012 8:52:04 PM] Tina Cummins: I can't get the nose and hair right...Flashface...

2nd sketch I did for Patsy
Photo courtesy of Tanya Cotrell on September 1st, 2014, for comparison to my sketch.

The second sketch I sent to Darrell, he couldn't identify. He said it looked nothing like Patsy's ex-husband Larry. He said, "It does look like a Calloway, maybe their younger brother Jimmy, but I don't remember what he looked like then." Darrell said he couldn't remember what Gene looked like back then, but he was a lot heavier than Larry and very stocky. I reassured Darrell that the sketches weren't exact, but I saw what I saw and I had to stick to it. I also reiterated that I couldn't tell whether it was past, present, or future that I was seeing. When my mind gets stuck on something relating to a murderer, it's like a pit bull and won't let go. Shellee can vouch for that. We've argued over many cases, only to find out later that we were both right, just unable to put our readings together. That's happened on more than one occasion. We're a great team. I told Darrell, the man I see inside the trailer was about 6' tall with brown hair. He was stocky built and taller and heavier than the other man. He had a bit of a pot belly. He had a brown beard and mustache with longer hair.

I didn't want to hurt Darrell's feelings with the information I got. Seeing that stuff in my mind brings me terrible nightmares and sometimes I force myself to block it out. I told Darrell, "I'm not always accurate, but when I am, I'm right on a dime." Darrell told me that my reading made sense to him, but it still didn't answer the question of whether or not Larry was involved. If the man in the car with Debra was a witness to the crime somehow, where did Larry Calloway fit into all of this? Was Larry the man in the car or someone else, maybe Jimmy? Was Gene the one in the trailer or was it Larry? All I know is what images popped into my mind back during that first reading.

I wanted to know what Debra Calloway and Gene Calloway looked like in person, because all I had were these flashes in my mind. Darrell said he would send me pictures. When I looked at the photos of Gene and Debra Calloway that clinched it for me. I knew in my mind they were the killers. When I looked at Gene Calloway, I saw evil staring back at me.

Photo courtesy of Darrell Kessinger
Debra Calloway Lt, Vernon Gene Calloway Rt

Chapter Three: The Disappearance of Patsy

Patricia Ann Kessinger Calloway was born on June 20th, 1954. She was 38-years-old at the time of her disappearance. Patsy was the mother of three grown children and a hard-working nurse's assistant. Her ex-husband was still living with her when she went missing, but he already had a child with another young girl named Shirley and was still seeing both of them. Larry was apparently stringing both women along.

Darrell Kessinger said he last spoke to his sister Patsy on February 26, 1993. He said Patsy told him, she was going turn her ex-husband Larry and his brother Gene in to the police for burning down her house. According to Darrell, she told him she was tired of his nonsense and wanted to move on because Larry wouldn't stop running around on her. Patsy wanted more out of life than a cheating husband. He'd already gotten the young girl pregnant once and she recently learned that Shirley was pregnant for the second time. Darrell said he begged Patsy not to turn the brothers in to the police, because he was afraid something bad would happen to her. Darrell states "Patsy was very much in love with her ex-husband Larry, and she didn't want him to leave her." She was holding that arson over Larry's head to keep him from leaving her for the girl. Darrell also said, "Patsy was a very loving person who was easily led. That's why she stayed with him after he had the first child with the other girl." According to Darrell, for the entire year after she filed for divorce, Patsy was emotionally hurt and began threatening her ex-husband Larry.

Patsy's desperation may very well have been the reason behind her disappearance, but I wouldn't know until I pursued it further. Did her ex-husband Larry want her out of the way because of the girl, or did the brothers or one brother, murder her to keep her silent? What happened to Patsy and who is responsible? At this point, the fact of the arson was easy to confirm, but I needed more details.

Once Patsy found out that Shirley was pregnant for the 2nd time, she decided to finally be rid of him. I believe Patsy was unaware that the 2nd child had been born, shortly before her disappearance. Prior to Patsy going missing, she decided to follow through with her threat, but she never got the opportunity to speak with police. The following week she went missing after she spoke to her brother and told him of her plans.

Once I confirmed the arson, I knew that both brothers had a motive for murder, so this is why Darrell couldn't decide if one or both were responsible for her disappearance. There is the possibility that someone else did something to Patsy and I couldn't rule that out yet. There is also the possibility that she just walked off because of circumstance. That's the position the police initially took when she disappeared. Because of my visuals and the length of time she'd been gone, I knew it was something far more sinister. Patsy was last seen on March 3rd, 1993 with Vernon Gene Calloway, her ex-husband's older brother.

I spoke to Ruby Renee Calloway on September 2nd, 2014. She is the daughter of Shirley and Larry Calloway. She told me that when Patsy went missing, she was already a couple of months old. So Darrell wasn't aware that Larry's girlfriend had already given birth to their second child at that point, nor was Patsy.

Chapter Four: The Circumstances

I mentioned earlier that Patsy was a nursing assistant. She worked at the Professional Care Home and Rehabilitation Center in Hartford, Kentucky. She was last seen at her work by co-workers around 10:30a.m., the morning of her disappearance. According to her work supervisor, Patsy said, "I have an emergency at home." She asked to leave work. Then she stated "I have to leave and I'll explain later."

As a journalist, I contacted a couple of employees who'd worked there and confirmed this.

First Patsy walks outside into the parking lot. Then she comes back in a few minutes later. She was visibly upset. Gene Calloway, the ex-brother-in-law, was seen holding a newspaper. Witnesses say it was a newspaper that contained information about a marriage license between Patsy's live-in, ex-husband Larry and the young girl, Shirley. I confirmed that the couple filed for marriage license on February 22, 1993 in Davies County, KY. The marriage license announcement was posted in the Messenger Inquirer out of Owensboro, KY, to run during the week of February 28th – March 6th, 1993. According to Darrell, a witness, Cindy Lykens, saw Patsy leave with "Gene" Calloway, Larry's brother, and get into his black, 1978 Chevrolet Blazer. Patsy was never heard from again, but her story didn't end there. Reports also circulated that Patsy was seeing walking down highway SR231, headed towards Beaver Dam, KY.

So Patsy was living with her philandering ex-husband who had gotten this young girl Shirley pregnant for the second time. Shirley had just recently given birth. Yes, he and Patsy were already divorced, but they still lived together. I learned that on the day Patsy filed for divorce from Larry, he deeded the remaining property over to Patsy, as noted in the arson case. That happened on March 3rd, 1992, the day she filed for divorce. That could've been a motive for revenge. Patsy was blackmailing him over the arson and possibly made a deal with him to keep silent about the arson, it could've been the reason he deeded the property over to her. At that time, both men had motive for wanting Patsy gone, but Larry more than Gene.

Back to square one. With Gene in my mind as the killer, I needed to find out what role Larry played and if he was the one in the car outside of her trailer with Debra.

Timeline:

November 10th, 1990, Nicholas Phelps was born to Larry and Shirley.

August 1st, 1991, the brothers committed the arson and Gene burned down Patsy's house.

February 1992, Patsy learns of the 2nd pregnancy.

March 2nd, 1992, Patsy filed for divorce from Larry Ray Calloway. The same day, he deeds the remainder of the property over to Patsy.

October 1st, 1992, Ruby Renee Calloway was born.

At this time, Patsy and Larry were still living together although he was seeing the young girl who'd had two of his children.

March 3rd, 1993 Patsy disappears.

Patsy was seen leaving her work with Gene Calloway, her ex-husband's older brother at 10:30a.m, according to witness Cindy Lykens.

Around 2:30pm she was seen walking toward Beaver Dam, KY, according to Mildred Calloway.

TO HAVE AND TO HOLD the above described real estate, together with all of the rights and privileges thereunto belonging or in anywise appertaining unto the SECOND PARTY, her heirs and assigns forever, with Covenant of GENERAL WARRANTY.

The parties hereto state the consideration reflected in this deed is the full consideration paid for the property. The SECOND PARTY joins this deed for the sole purpose of certifying the consideration pursuant to KRS Chapter 382.

IN TESTIMONY WHEREOF, witness the signatures of the FIRST PARTY and SECOND PARTY on this, the day and date first hereinabove written.

FIRST PARTY:

Larry Ray Calloway
LARRY RAY CALLOWAY

SECOND PARTY:

Patricia Ann Calloway
PATRICIA ANN CALLOWAY

COMMONWEALTH OF KENTUCKY)
                        (sct
COUNTY OF OHIO   )

The foregoing Deed and Consideration Certificate was acknowledged and sworn to before me by Larry Ray Calloway, a married person whose wife is Patricia Ann Calloway, FIRST PARTY, on this the _5_ day of _March_____, 1992.

_____
NOTARY PUBLIC, State at Lg. Ky
My commission expires: _1/25/96_

Photocopy courtesy of Darrell Kessinger

As I stated before, three weeks passed and law enforcement believed that Patsy was upset about the marriage license and just walked away from her life. That wasn't an unreasonable prospect for the first day she went missing or even the first couple of days. After all, she was already divorced and this man was with another girl that she knew about. After a couple of days, I have to ask myself, "why not start looking into this?" "Why didn't they take this seriously?" When

Patsy first found out about Larry's affair with the young girl, she was beaten to a pulp by two women after a confrontation ensued. Well get back to that later, but for now let's talk about her walking down that road. Is it true? Did Patsy just walk away from her life? Because of what I saw in my head, I knew that wasn't true.

A witness, sister of Larry and Gene Calloway, made a statement to police. She thought she saw Patsy walking on Highway 231 heading towards Beaver Dam on the day she went missing. From this perspective it appears Patsy was angry and distraught about the marriage license and was walking, perhaps out to clear her head. If Patsy was walking down that road, anyone could've taken her or an accident may have happened. I had to stick with my gut instinct and visuals so this didn't make sense to me.

I asked Patsy's brother, "If she was walking down the street, she couldn't have been "last seen with Gene?" This doesn't wash unless Gene was walking down the street with her. Darrell said Patsy's missing poster looks as if it was written up prior to her disappearance. She can't be "last seen with Gene" and then be "seen walking towards Beaver Dam." According to Darrell Kessinger, the witness, Mildred Calloway, said she pulled over to talk to Patsy and offer her a ride. Then she realized it was Gene Calloway's wife Debra, wearing a black wig; a nurse's uniform; and a brown jacket or coat. This is the description of Patsy as she appeared when she left work that day.

Darrell said the witness, their sister Mildred, told him that Debra was "disguised as Patsy." If that's the case, why didn't Mildred tell that to police? She initially told police it was Patsy. According to Darrell, another sister-in-law of Debra Calloway told him that Debra asked her to dispose of the wig she wore that day. Darrell said she told him she disposed of it in a WalMart bag.

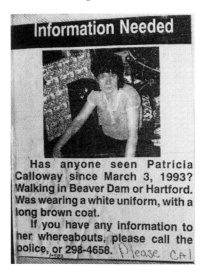

Information Needed

Has anyone seen Patricia Calloway since March 3, 1993? Walking in Beaver Dam or Hartford. Was wearing a white uniform, with a long brown coat.
If you have any information to her whereabouts, please call the police, or 298-4658. Please cal

It is uncertain if or where she disposed of the wig. When I called Mildred, she refused to speak to me. The other sister, Vicki Hoheimer, contacted me on September 28th, 2012, and reports that these accusations by Kessinger are completely false regarding the wig. Vicki told me that she'd never disposed of a wig, but she did admit to seeing a wig in Debra's possession at Debra's house. Vicki insisted Darrell was lying and Debra never asked her to dispose of it. So I wondered, was Patsy really walking down the road, or was this woman in disguise to make it appear that she was? With conflicting stories from the women, it's hard to know. If the later was the case, then why lie to police? That's obstruction of justice. Does the blood of kin trump the rights of a murder victim and family member? Patsy was still the mother of their niece and nephew. Where does conscience abide in the minds of these people?

I asked Darrell, "When did Patsy first get reported missing? He said she was reported missing from the very first day. That struck me as odd, so I made a note of it in my journal. Normally, unless it is a child; elderly; or mentally challenged person that's missing, it doesn't even get reported until after they've been gone for 24 hours. I wanted to know, "Why the urgency?" Darrell couldn't answer that without speculation.

He explained to me that at the time of his sister's disappearance, he was in the army and was stuck in Arkansas. He wasn't able to get back to KY until almost three weeks after she was gone, so what happened in those first weeks was a mystery to him.

I asked Darrell, "Who reported her missing?" He said, "Larry did." From the first moment, her ex-husband went to the police immediately. This struck me as out of the ordinary. What interest does an ex-husband have in his ex-wife's disappearance? After all, he's leaving her and getting married to another woman, who just months earlier, delivered their second child, Ruby Renee. He may have to explain things to Patsy, but why run to police immediately, unless you know something? Usually the spouse is the first suspect or person of interest. It seems that was the case with Patsy Calloway, once the police realized she wasn't coming back. I had to find out more. Was her ex-husband Larry setting up an alibi that day, or was he genuinely concerned for her safety?"

Darrell Kessinger, Patsy's brother, went to Hartford Kentucky on March 23rd, 1993, in search of answers. He spoke with some of Patsy's co-workers, who said they hadn't been questioned by police about her disappearance yet. How could this be? She'd been missing for twenty days by the time he came to Kentucky. Didn't the police want to know the circumstances around her disappearance? This is how Darrell learned about them. Darrell Kessinger then began pushing the police department for answers. This coincides with what Larry later told me, that he wasn't getting any help from the police, despite going over there numerous times.

Okay so Maryanne already knows her sister Shirley and Larry are planning to get married. So why would she care if Patsy left with Gene? Why would she care so much that she'd lose pay and leave her job to tell them? What did they know? Perhaps she just wanted to tell them that Patsy knew of their plans, but couldn't she just call them? Maybe they didn't have a phone. Again, why the urgency, or was it a cover up to give an alibi? Darrell said that Maryanne told him she left to make sure Patsy didn't leave work to go beat up Shirley. Still, I made a mental note of these questions. From this point, if Patsy left her work with Gene, what happened next? Where did Larry go after Maryanne told them? Aside from going to police, that is one of the biggest mysteries of this case.

Chapter Five: Patsy's Trailer

Things were falling into place with my visuals. I asked Darrell if Patsy had a trailer. He said she did and it was exactly as I had described to him. I asked him if law enforcement ever searched in or around Patsy's trailer for her remains, because of my visuals. He said, "No, they never searched it." So the police didn't question the employees at the nursing home or search her own home? Darrell said, "Nope." That made no sense to me. You've got a woman that disappeared, arson, and a threat of murder. I thought that maybe, the police already knew or suspected what had happened to Patsy and that she was in fact, deceased. They had to know something about that trailer otherwise why wouldn't they search her home for clues? Darrell said he wanted the trailer searched. After all it was her home and "You'd think that would be the first place the police searched."

Darrell said he spoke to the current owner of the trailer, John Lindley, and got permission to search the property and the trailer. Of course, this was nineteen years later. Darrell told me that friends of his from the Jodi Powers Search and Rescue Technologies and Tennessee K-9 Search and Rescue had gone out to the trailer where Patsy lived and conducted some searches. He said that he was very grateful to Mr. Lindley for allowing them to search. He said Mr. Lindley actually came with them on one occasion and helped them. Darrel said, "That man didn't know me from shoe or shinola, but he just jumped right into help. Mr. Lindley was extremely supportive."

Scott Heltsley works with Tennessee K-9 Search and Rescue as a searcher and cadaver dog handler. Scott said that his dog Bear (a trained cadaver dog with 4 prior years of experience) had gone into the trailer, walked directly into the bathroom, and sat down. For those of you unaware, when a cadaver dog does this, it is considered a positive "hit" that a death occurred in that spot. Darrell said the dog also made a positive hit on Patsy's bedroom, on the same wall as the bathroom, opposite side. Others from the JPRST were there when Bear made the positive hit. Darrell told me that an instructor in forensics came out there with a group of students and sprayed Alumina and Blue Star on the trailer. She volunteered her services to Darrell and also accompanied the group on a separate occasion and found blood spatter in the trailer.

Photo of bathroom courtesy of
Darrell Kessinger

He said she told him it was positive for blood. This was confirmed through emails the two shared. The instructor called it a "smoking gun." According to Scott Heltsley of TN K-9 S&R, and Chris Williams of the JPRST, they asked the woman if she should be doing that. Since blood was found in the trailer, they should've backed off and called police. That's what they both said they told her, they wanted to do.

Darrell said that Chris Williams called local and county police officials to alert them of their findings, but the police didn't seem concerned with it. After all, it was 19 years after her disappearance. Who knows where the blood came from? All of the people at the trailer were under the impression that the trailer was cleared by police to search and they did so with permission. Why haven't the police ever searched the Patsy's trailer?

I learned that Patsy's daughter, Tanya Cotrell, lived in the trailer for a few years after her mother's disappearance. For the first six or so months, she said her brother Shane lived there. She said she moved into the trailer in December of 1993 or January of 1994. Tanya told me that in the Summer of 1994, they noticed a bad smell around the back door of the trailer, the following Summer. She said it smelled like something died there. She said they thought an animal had crawled up under the trailer and died. According to Tanya, they never noticed the blood. Darrell gave me copies of many photos of what was obviously blood inside of Patsy's trailer. The majority of it was under the linoleum. Most of it had been cleaned up and what they found was brought out by the Alumina and Blue Star.

There was a large streak of blood spatter on the bathroom door, but the bulk of it was on the bathroom floor and wall. There was blood on the living room ceiling panels and on the floor just outside and behind the bathroom door. The hallway carpet had been previously torn out, but some of the linoleum remained. Underneath the remaining linoleum were the large blood stains. Portions of the walls had been cut out and removed prior to examination of the trailer. The blood had seeped down into the plywood underneath.

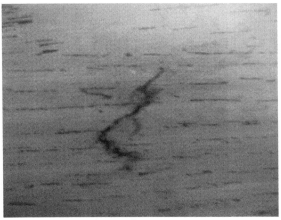

Photo courtesy of Darrell Kessinger

I'll ask again, "Why would you find all of this information, and the police not search her trailer?" Darrell said it made no sense to him. He said he'd posed that question to the detective who was now investigating the case. He said Sargent Bryan Whittaker told him, "Why would I go out there and search that trailer? The only thing that would prove is that she's dead." If that comment by the detective is true, my thought is, "It's what you're paid to do." If someone goes out anywhere and finds human blood spatter, my impression is that the police should check it out. Am I wrong?

At the time I realized the officer was speaking in terms of evidence, but the way he put it to Patsy's brother was less than professional. I couldn't believe that an officer would speak to a grieving family member like that, but his statements were confirmed by Belinda Powers and Chris Williams of the JPRST. However, testing that blood spatter for DNA would give police a positive identification if it was in fact Patsy's blood. If it's not hers, then who's blood is in that trailer? Did the officer know something he wasn't sharing? Probably.

The more Darrell told me about the circumstances surrounding Patsy's disappearance, the more questions I had. Darrell told me that his sister Patsy had disappeared exactly one year to the day of her divorce filing from her now ex-husband Larry. Now in my mind, I was almost certain that Larry wasn't the culprit for the physical murder of Patsy. But because she disappeared on that anniversary, it would give police even more reason to suspect him.

For me, this posed the question that he may have been set-up for appearances sake or involved in the planning. I needed to find out. The only way we were going to get any factual information is if the witnesses talked. So, I set out on a mission to interview the pertinent witnesses that would agree to discuss the case. This would also insure the accuracy of my article to the best of my ability. I told Darrell that the only way I could write the article from a journalistic perspective, was to hear their side of the story. With that, Darrell gave me their contact information.

Timeline:

1989, Patsy learns that her husband Larry is cheating on her and a fight ensues between her and two women.
1990 Shirley, Larry's girlfriend, delivers a son.
August 1st, 1991, Patsy's house is burned down by Gene Calloway because he was paid to by Larry.
August 1991, Patsy begins threatening Larry over the arson to keep him from leaving her.

March 3rd, 1992, Patsy files for divorce after she learns Shirley is pregnant for the 2nd time. Larry deeds remainder of property over to Patsy.

March 3rd, 1993 Patsy disappears. Patsy was seen leaving her work with Gene Calloway, her ex-husband's older brother at 10:30a.m, according to witness Cindy Lykens.

Around 2:30pm she was seen walking toward Beaver Dam, KY, according to Mildred Calloway.

June 1994, Tanya Cotrell notices awful smell in the trailer by the bathroom and back door, because of the heat.

2012, Trailer is searched with cadaver dog and the dog makes a positive hit. Blood spatter is discovered about the trailer.

Chapter Six: An Eye-Witness Account

A week after our initial conversations, I informed Darrell that it was going to take some time for me to contact all the potential witnesses in Patsy's case prior to running an article. Darrell said he had recently spoken to some of the Calloway family and his suspicions of his sister's murder were confirmed. He said he had contacted them many times over the years, and they finally agreed to sit down and discuss Patsy's case with him. According to Darrell, Larry Calloway did not want to be recorded or go on the record. Jimmy Calloway, Larry and Gene's younger brother, confirmed that his oldest brother Vernon Gene had murdered Patsy and buried her remains. The following statements are according to Darrell Kessinger and reflect a conversation he had with the two men:

According to statements made by Jimmy Calloway to Darrell Kessinger, he'd seen Patsy's deceased body between 11:30 a.m. – 12:30 p.m. the day she disappeared, in the back of his brother Gene Calloway's, black Chevy Blazer. He described trash bags in the back of his brother's truck. It has not been confirmed if Jimmy made a complete statement to the Kentucky State Police, but according to Darrell, Jimmy told him that he felt the trash bag. He said he moved his hand down the trash back and felt a shoulder. Jimmy said he continued to move his hands down the trash bag until he got to what felt like a head. He then tore open the trash bag and saw Patricia Calloway's body.

According to Darrell Kessinger, Jimmy Calloway told Darrell that Patsy was laying on her left side; one eye still open; and her wind pipe had been cut. He said she was still wearing her nurse's uniform. He stated that the carpet in the back of the truck was saturated with blood. Jimmy said that he later saw that the carpet had been torn out of the Chevy Blazer. He also said he saw the carpet remnants in his brother Gene's trash cans. Jimmy said when he touched the carpet, it was saturated with blood. This confirmed for me that he was the witness I was seeing and that the murder had taken place as I had seen in my mind's eyes. I still wasn't certain if Larry had helped in the planning or not, but the case was going where it needed to go. Who was the 2nd man sitting in the car with Debra?

Kentucky State Police official Sargent Bryan Whittaker confirmed that Jimmy Calloway had taken three polygraphs and passed all three exams. Sargent Whittaker also stated that Larry Calloway failed his polygraph exam and Gene Calloway passed his. According to Darrell, Detective Phillip Ballard, one of the original investigating officers stated, "Gene Calloway threatened to cut Patricia Calloway's throat from ear to ear." This was later confirmed. He said that Gene also told police to "Prove it," basically daring the police to catch him. Gene allegedly made that same statement to a witness as well.

Darrell said that Jimmy and Gene Calloway passed their polygraph examinations and that Larry had failed. This much was confirmed by Detective Bryan Whittaker who was now working the case. However, witnesses told Darrell, that Gene was bragging about taking Valium on the day he took his polygraph exam, and that he did kill Patsy. How could this be? If Larry had nothing to do with the killing how could he fail the polygraph? Maybe all isn't what it seemed, so I pushed on.

Now the plot thickens once again. I realize that polygraphs aren't full proof, but why would a man go directly to police when he finds out his brother took off somewhere with his ex-wife? Why would that same man fail a polygraph in regard to the disappearance of his ex-wife, who just happened to disappear on the anniversary of her filing for divorce? What did Larry know that he wasn't telling police? Did he help plan it or was he set up? Was his sister's girlfriend unknowingly giving him and alibi, or was she in fear for her sister safety?

According to Darrell, neither Larry nor Jimmy Calloway claim knowledge of where their brother Vernon Gene buried Patsy's remains. He said Jimmy gave him very undescriptive directions, but he didn't know the exact burial spot. **How could Jimmy give them directions to her remains if he wasn't there?**

Darrell and I were discussing this spot on Google maps and I came up with a coordinate for him in regard to the information he gave me from Jimmy. The suspected spot happened to be a farm belonging to a man named Andy Anderson that I'd already mentioned. The spot is Southwest from Patsy's trailer, where I was being pulled to from the beginning of my readings. Anyway, Darrell claims the three men met in front of the Hartford Community Center where Patsy's car was located, so they could tell him what happened to his sister.

I asked Darrell Kessinger, "Did police find any evidence or scene of a murder anywhere? Darrell stated to me that initially, no evidence was collected from law enforcement that he knew of, because they assumed Patsy had just left. He said that his sister's case was blundered from day one. He also didn't believe that Larry went straight to police like he claims. So at this point, we have multiple witnesses that may or may not be credible; an eye-witness to the deceased body of Patsy; and multiple suspects who are all related to the victim.

If what Darrell Kessinger claims is true about the eye-witness, why aren't the police arresting the murderer? Darrell said that he asked Detective Whittaker that and he was told that Jimmy's testimony would never hold up in front of a jury. Darrell said he told the officer, "He's illiterate, but he's not mentally retarded. I had to find out for myself. Is it because there wasn't enough evidence at this time to corroborate the eye-witness account? What if anything were the police told about her disappearance? I needed to know so I set out to interview the most pertinent witnesses I could find, Mr. Larry Calloway, Patsy's ex-husband

and potential murderer, and Mr. Gene Calloway, suspected murderer and ex-brother-in-law to the victim.

Chapter Seven: Persons Of Interest, Speech Analysis

My first attempt at an interview was to contact the man at the very core of the investigation, Mr. Vernon Gene Calloway. After all, he was the last person seen with her according to witnesses. I called his home phone number. A woman answered the phone and I suspect it was Debra Calloway. I introduced myself as a photojournalist for MPN. I told them I wondered if they would answer a few questions for me in regard to the disappearance of Patsy Calloway. The woman hung up on me. I expected that reaction from his camp. Later that day, I got a call back from that same Calloway residence as identified on my caller ID, from a woman telling me to "fuck off." I was told, "Leave this investigation alone or you could be next." That second phone call answered a lot of questions for me. When someone bites so defensively at someone they've never met, they're hiding something.

Next, I proceeded to call the home of Larry Calloway. If I was going to get anywhere with this article, he needed to talk to me. His current wife and then girlfriend Shirley Calloway answered the phone. I explained to her who I was and that I was writing an article for MissingPersonsNews about Patsy. Shirley asked Larry if he wanted to speak with me and then told me I would have to call back a few hours later. He wasn't working and I could hear him in the background. I'm sure my call startled him and he wasn't expecting it. After all, it had been nineteen years since Patsy went missing. Perhaps he wanted time to collect his thoughts or get his story straight. I called back a few hours later, but this time Larry answered the phone. He said he couldn't talk right now and asked me to call back in a couple days. He did agree to the interview but they said he was ill at the moment and would have to do it later.

I waited two days and made the call. Speech analysis is a large part of interviewing a person. It is one way journalists get down to the truth and is commonly used in law enforcement. At first, Larry was Stonewall Jackson and not giving me much. I had to season him a while in order cook him later. I commiserated with this potential killer and in my mind suspected sex-offender, to find out what I could. I told him that my family was from Hazard and I know how it is to live life in the hills. I told him I was in my late 30s and a very young grandma. I explained to him that our interest was strictly to find any information we can about Patsy's whereabouts and I could only publish an article if I had his side of the story.

I said to Larry with a Southern draw, "You see, in the city, everybody sees everythang, but nobody knows nothin. In the country, nobody sees nothin, but everybody knows everythang. Which is it for you Larry?" He said, "Yeah, yeah… I know what you mean." With that, the interview proceeded. I talked and flirted with him a bit to get what I could get out of him. In journalism and missing persons' cases, it's like that. It's a cat and mouse game. If you want to get the truth, you've got to use what you've got. I needed his cooperation if I was going to get anywhere near the truth of what happened to Patsy. The following statements are portions of the interview with Mr. Larry Calloway that was recorded:

I said, "Do you have any idea of what happened to your ex-wife?"
Larry said, "<u>Heh. No, I really don't</u>. I've heard so many dag gone stories, that I don't know what to believe."

When he uses "Heh" this indicates hesitation and thinking of an answer. He follows this by "No, I really don't." Using the word really in this situation is inappropriate and is indicative of a lie. Now, my interview was after Darrell had met with Larry and his brother at the community center, so he starts off the interview with a lie. His brother Jimmy already told him he'd seen Patsy's body, so he did have an idea of what happened to her. Then Larry backs it up with "I've heard so many dag gone stories" to try and cover up the lie and only partially reveal the truth. It is common for criminals to mix lies with the truth. He doesn't know what I know and he's thinking about it, so I question him immediately.

Cummins: "Did you ever meet with Darrell and tell him that your brother Gene killed Patsy?"
Calloway: "I met with him and we discussed that and <u>I said I don't know who killed her, if she's dead.</u>"

"I said I don't know who killed her, if she's dead." According to statement analysis, this direct statement indicates that he's telling the truth in regard to her murder, but I would need further confirmation, because he could just be recalling the conversation he had with Darrell. Also, people without a conscience have no trouble telling lies. He could also be revealing a controlling tendency to let me know, he's on top of what he says. He was definitely paying attention to my questions and his answers.

Cummins: "Darrell Kessinger said you met with him at the Hartford Community Center and that you and your brother Jimmy said that Gene had killed Patsy."

I included him purposely in that question to see if Larry would admit to knowledge of the murder.

Cummins: He corrected me stating, (Calloway) "I said nothing. Jimmy is a witness for 'em if it ever comes to court."

At this point, Larry is letting me know that he knows what I'm up to and in search of answers. He gives me a direct recall statement of his conversation at the community center, but doesn't fall for the bait.

Cummins: "What about your brother Jimmy. I heard he's on trial, is that true?"
Calloway: "Yeah, he's their main witness."

I was asking Larry about Jimmy in regard to Jimmy's trial but Larry's mind took him back to Patsy's case and he stated "he's their main witness." This is a red flag for me because he's contemplating what he's going to say next. So I continue with the questioning about his brother Jimmy and state the question clearly.

Cummins: "And he's on trial for what? Rape?"
Calloway: "Uh no. It was a… oh heck. It's been so long. He's been going to court so dag gone long, I don't really remember."

The word really, used in this way is an indication that he does remember but is lying to cover it. If he didn't remember, normal speech calls for him saying, "I don't remember." Placing the word "really" indicates a deceit, and that he does remember somewhat, so I question him on it.

Cummins: "You don't remember what he's been charged with?"
Calloway: "No. See, I've had a stroke, and all my memory has been lost. I've lost a lot of my memory."

This confirms the prior lie. First he says he's lost all of his memory, then he says he's lost "a lot" of it. I didn't want to frighten him off, so I switched gears.

Cummins: "Gene is the one that's married to Debra, right?"
Calloway: "Uh, yeah."
Cummins: "OK, is Debra, is she the one who wore the wig?"
Calloway: "Now, that's what they say, I don't know." "Nothings ever been proven, so I don't know." "That's one of the stories I've heard, see I have… they claimed she walked through Hartford to Beaver Dam. See. I walked through every gas station, store, gas station and showed her pictures and stuff. See I was the one out searching. The law wasn't searching. I was. And that's another thing. I had no help from his family during this time."

When asked about the wig, Larry answers with "I don't know." This is a direct statement that is most likely accurate. He starts out with what he's heard and follows up with what he's heard. He then states, "see I have…" Then he stops that statement and continues with "they claimed she walked through Hartford to Beaver Dam." In this moment, Larry is recalling when being questioned about the wig? Did he know about the wig? I suspect this is the case. He stopped himself before he revealed what he knew. Who is the "they" he's referring to? Was it his sisters? Was it the killers? I suspect it was both. Then he shows defensiveness when he speaks of the law and Patsy's family. Where they accusing him of harming Patsy? Was his guilty conscience speaking for him? He is also diverting attention away from the question at hand. Instead of answering my direct question about the wig, he goes into defensive mode which is a red flag for me. If he's innocent, why does he go into defensive mode? Since he was already so defensive, I changed directions again.

Cummins: "Yeah, Darrell said he was in the military. He was gone."
Calloway: "He was in the military, but he was in Arkansas. He came in that Summer, or that Winter and was gonna help me and he didn't help me. They stayed a couple days, and they went back."
Cummins: "Darrell said he doesn't blame you."
Calloway: "He said, yeah, as far as I'm concerned, me and Darrell are still friends."
Cummins: "Yeah, he said he's met with you and your brother Jimmy. What he's concerned about is finding his sister's remains."
Calloway: "<u>Me too. I want her found</u>."

At this point, Larry is beginning to relax after he doesn't feel attacked. He begins to get less defensive. When Larry says, "I want her found," this was a direct statement indicating that he didn't know where Patsy was located. He could've just been sizing me up and trying to convince me of an untruth.

Cummins: "Darrell said that the police never searched the trailer where you lived with Patsy. Is that correct?"
Calloway: "Not that I can remember they didn't. They came out there and searched my vehicles."

For someone who claimed they lost all their memory or some of their memory, Larry's memory seems intact. Why would police search his vehicles, but not the trailer? What did the police suspect? Remember, this is the beginning of the investigation. Patsy had only just gone missing and they hadn't begun investigating yet. Perhaps they didn't have permission to search it. Without knowing circumstances surrounding the disappearance of Patsy, they had no probable cause for a warrant.

Cummins: "They searched your vehicles. Did they say anything about them?"
Calloway: "No. Un Huh. Everything. I'm the one who went to the police when she was missing."

This confirms what Darrell had told me about Larry going to police, but I'd already confirmed that with the officer by the time of our interview.

Cummins: "Ok. So, when did you go to the police?"
Calloway: "Same day. I couldn't find her. She didn't come home. I called her daughter in Indiana to see if she'd come up there and if she did, to call. And I went to police about three times that day, cause I couldn't even find her car. And when I did find her car, it was sitting right there in town. And the chief of police told

me, "Go up there and bring it over to the police station. And I did."

Tanya Cotrell, Patsy and Larry's daughter, confirmed that her dad in fact called her in Indiana. Interesting, that he refers to his own daughter by saying, "her daughter." Psychologically speaking, why would he disassociate himself with his own daughter? So again, why the urgency and why go to the police? If he was just worried about Patsy being angry with him about the marriage license, he'd have no reason to go to the police. He had to suspect that something terrible had happened to Patsy or even that something was planned to happen to Patsy. Was he aware of a murder plot? Had there been a threat to him about Patsy? What made him go to the police three times that day? Was he setting up an alibi for himself?

You don't go to police because you're afraid your ex-wife left you because you're going to marry someone else. He uses the word "even" improperly when he states, "'cause I couldn't <u>even</u> find her car." Normal speech calls for him to say, "because, I couldn't find her car." This could be indicative of deceit. He also says he went to the police, "Same day." Why wouldn't he wait for her to come home that night to talk to her?

Cummins: "The police told you to bring the car to the police station?"
Calloway: "<u>Yes they did</u>."

That's a direct statement indicating truth.

Cummins: "Wow. Where did you find the keys?"
Calloway: "<u>Ah, they was in the floor</u>."
Cummins: "Ok, so the keys were in the floor. You got

the car and took it over to the police station?"
Calloway: "<u>Yeah, it was only about a block, half a block, right there</u>."

If the police suspected Larry that day of committing a crime against Patsy, they wouldn't have sent him to go get Patsy's car and bring it to them. Furthermore, they would've asked to search her trailer. This confirms that the police initially thought Patsy had just walked off from her life. But it still doesn't explain why Larry went to the police in the first place, unless he was in fear of something bad happening to Patsy at the hands of his brother Gene. Did he know about the plot to kill her? Why didn't he just go over to Gene's house? He knew Patsy left her work with him. Why would he say "they" said she was walking up in Beaver Dam? Did Mildred tell him that, or was he lying to try and cover his own tracks? When asked about the wig, he refers to "them" telling him she was seen walking toward Beaver Dam. He's obviously lying about the wig and Patsy walking, but why?

Chapter Eight: Discussing the Arson

Cummins: "OK, so you were charged with arson. You had your brother burn down the house for the insurance money, right?"
Calloway: "Exactly. And <u>I'm the one who turned state's evidence. I turned myself in</u>."
Cummins: "You turned yourself in? You turned state's evidence and he got off? He was acquitted?"
Calloway: "<u>Exactly. I turned myself in. I turned the arson in. I was trying to find her. I wanted her found</u>."
Cummins: "You wanted her found so you turned the arson in?"

Calloway: "<u>Yes. I wanted to know what happened to her. I wanted to know where she was.</u>"
Cummins: "Oh. That's a big difference. You wanted Patsy found, so you told the police."
Calloway: "<u>Yeah, cause everybody was accusing me and such, so I, you know, the detectives, so.</u>"

Larry's direct statement was confirmed that he in fact turned himself into police for the August 1991 arson of the house he shared with Patsy. He and Gene were indicted for arson on June 10th, 1993. The grand jury deliberated in a hearing the week earlier. In his statement to me, he directly stated that he wanted Patsy found. Did he know about Gene's intent to kill Patsy and then have 2nd thoughts about it? Did he help plan it?

Darrell Kessinger claims that he was going to be caught for the arson because items from the burned house had been recovered elsewhere. However, the clear statements Larry made indicate truthfulness on his part according to speech analysis. This was also confirmed with law enforcement. Items from that arson were recovered a year after Larry had turned himself in to police. It does however contradict his statement that he had "no idea" of what happened to Patsy. I believe Larry knew of his brother's plan to kill Patsy or him and his girlfriend Shirley were both threatened by Gene in some way.

When I spoke with his daughter Tanya, she told me that when they got money from the insurance policy from the arson, they spent the money. He put some money down on a new trailer. He and Shirley bought some furniture and also used some money to buy the land for the trailer. Gene was paid his $1,000. But where did Patsy figure into all of this. It was her house! I believe Patsy blackmailed Larry into signing over the deed to the property, the day she filed for divorce. As far as Gene goes, he had something on Larry and Shirley besides the arson in my opinion. Otherwise why would he threaten them? With Patsy gone, the threat of jail was eliminated, unless he was involved or if Gene had something else on them. Shirley told me that Gene said, "If I go down, you're all going down with me." I questioned Larry on why police were accusing him if they had the information about the arson.

Cummins: "They were accusing you?"
Calloway: "No no. They were accusing Vernon… Gene. Yeah. They were saying that it had to be him. So I turned state's evidence… turned it in, states evidence against him."

Less than a minute earlier in our interview, Larry said that the police were accusing him and that's why he turned the arson in to police and that he wanted Patsy found. Now he said they were accusing Vernon Gene. He's contradicting himself. Was he afraid of Gene? Did he need a legitimate excuse for talking to police so Gene wouldn't come after him? Was he trying to get his brother jailed so he could feel safe? Or did he just want to point the finger at Gene to get it off of him? This is what I suspected. In my opinion, Patsy's murder was well thought out and he was involved with the planning and just needed an alibi.

Cummins: "When you and Jimmy met with Darrell Kessinger, your brother Jimmy is the one who

described seeing the body in the back of the truck?"
Calloway: "<u>Yeah</u>."

"Yeah" is a direct answer indicating truthfulness. He acknowledges that the conversation in fact took place and that Jimmy said he witnessed Patsy's body in the truck.

Cummins: "Did you ever confront your brother Gene about that?"
Calloway: "<u>I've asked him, you know, things, and I've never gotten an answer. And I've been waiting all this time for him to say something, slip up, anything.</u>"

When Larry says, "you know, things," he shows that he hesitated asking his brother directly if he killed Patsy and disposed of her. This too indicates he's being truthful that he doesn't know where Patsy's remains are. Otherwise why would he ask him anything? That doesn't mean he didn't help plan it out. If he was involved in her murder, he'd have no need to ask his brother anything about it unless it was to get their story straight or to know the details of it. It does show that he is afraid of his brother, otherwise why not just ask Gene directly? What are the "things" he's referring to? I suspect Larry found out about the murder shortly after it occurred or perhaps the same day. I believe he knew before-hand that Gene was planning it and maybe helped him plan it out.

Cummins: "So you didn't kill Patsy?"
Calloway: "<u>I would never harm a hair on her. I am the one who passed out flyers from here to Indiana. I took 'em to the police station. They didn't even know anything about it. I took 'em to the police station and</u>

everything else. <u>The way she, that she was supposedly seen walking</u>."

When Larry states, "I would never harm a hair on her," this indicates that he wouldn't in the future, but he has in the past. He didn't say, "I've never harmed a hair on her." This tells me two things. According to speech analysis, it confirms that he doesn't know factually that she's deceased because he uses future tense. He only knows what he's heard and that he has in fact been abusive to Patsy in the past. Would never indicates guilt for harming her. He didn't answer the direct question that was posed to him in a direct way, also indicating avoidance and guilt. He then becomes defensive and reverts back to what he's done to try and locate Patsy. He refers to his dealings with the police not believing him in that he had to bring missing persons flyers to them. Was this to get the police not to suspect him? Was it his intention to appear as the "dutiful" husband? He uses the word "<u>supposedly</u>" when referring to "them." I suspect he doesn't believe his sister or knows for a fact she is lying.

Based on speech analysis, Larry was trying to find his ex-wife, but he continues to take a defensive stance. I try to get him to relax and give me more information. What is he hiding? What does he know? What has he seen from his brother in the past that would make him be so fearful? What does Gene have on Larry? Did he help them plan Patsy's murder?

Cummins: "I can see where it makes you look bad, because you're her husband and you're having an affair with a young girl."
Calloway: "<u>Exactly. Well, I'm not… a young girl</u>

turned my head. It happens. It happens every day."
Cummins: "What about your sister Vicki?"
Calloway: "Now I don't know anything about her in this case to do with it or whatever.
Calloway: We don't associate. I found the car. Cause I'd already been to the police station two or three times and they said if I found the car, bring it to them. And when I found it, I went back up there and told 'em where it was, and they had me bring it right over there to the police station."

He admits his affair with Shirley makes him look guilty when he says, "exactly." Then he says, "Well, I'm not," but he stops himself before he completes that sentence. He's not what, a pedophile? A child rapist? I believe Gene Calloway intended to make him look guilty. Larry was the perfect scapegoat given the fact that she disappeared on the anniversary of their divorce, and the fact that he'd just gotten a marriage license to wed another woman who had just recently had a 2nd child with him. There is also the fact that Patsy was blackmailing him and he signed over the deed to the land on the day she filed for divorce. This was no coincidence. It was planned out almost to perfection. His brother Gene set him up to look guilty. Gene may have thought he was doing Larry a favor. He may have also been controlling Larry, or planning to kill him. I'm sure the set up was for Larry to take the heat off of Gene. If they all helped plan it, Larry could well be getting revenge on Patsy for having to sign over the deed to the property, and for her blackmailing him.

When asked about his sister Vicki earlier, he deflected the conversation back to the car. Did his sister see Debra in the car and did he know that she saw her?

Darrell had mentioned this to me once before and I suspect that is the case. That's probably the reason he doesn't associate with his sister Vicki, because he knows that she is hiding something. Maybe it had to do with the wig and the car. I believe Larry called his sister Mildred that day and I believe that his sister told him she saw Debra Calloway; dressed up as Patsy; driving her car. In my mind, this is what prompted Larry Calloway to go to police along with the possibility that he'd been threatened by Gene. Did he call Jimmy and did Jimmy tell him he'd seen Patsy's body? Did he know of the plot to kill Patsy? So again, I follow up with that question.

Cummins: "So what made you go to the police station to find your wife that day?"
Calloway: "Cause she didn't come home."

Although this was a direct statement by Larry, Patsy not coming home was only part of the reason he went to police. According to Larry, he went almost directly to the police after Maryanne paid him and Shirley a visit. Maryanne left work shortly after Patsy did. So if Larry had gone to Gene's house, he would've found them. Maybe he did and then went to police. However his statement indicates that he was concerned for her safety, again, so I follow up.

Cummins: "She didn't come home, so you didn't go to her work and look for her?"
Calloway: "I went by her work."
Cummins: "Did they tell you at that time she went with Gene?"
Calloway: "No I didn't go in. Now, I was at Shirley's house when this happened, when Gene supposedly went

to the nursing home."

It's interesting how defensive Larry is and he says, "Now I was at Shirley's house when this happened." When what happened Larry? What do you know that you're not sharing with the rest of the class? Then he corrects himself and says, "when Gene supposedly went to the nursing home." Okay, this makes no sense. Larry says he went to police because Patsy didn't come home. But then he claims he went by her work, but didn't go in. Why would he go by her work and not go in? Then he states he was at Shirley's house "when Gene supposedly went to the nursing home."

Was Larry lying to try and cover up where he went that day? Did he find Gene, Debra, and Patsy? Did he already know what was happening? If Larry was at Shirley's apartment when Gene went to the nursing home, how could he be waiting at his house for her to come home? That is a direct indication of deceit. He stated clearly that he went to police because she didn't come home, but yet he stated that he was at Shirley's house. Which is it?
I know now that he's lying about being at his home waiting so I follow up.

Cummins: "You were at your girlfriend's house when this happened?"
Calloway: "Yeah, in an apartment down here. It's a big complex."

Larry confirms that he was in fact at his girlfriend's apartment. So what made him run around and go looking for his ex-wife? Was he waiting for her at his house later that night? Again, I follow up to confirm.

Cummins: "Even though you were divorced or whatever, you were at your girlfriends? You were still living at the same house with her (Patsy) but you were divorced?"

Calloway: "<u>Exactly. And her sister works at the nursing home. Shirley's sister worked at the nursing home when my wife, ex-wife was. She come down there and told us Gene had showed her (Patsy) the paper and she had left the nursing home</u>."

When he says, "Exactly," he indicates that he was not at his home when Patsy went missing, but with his girlfriend at her apartment. He goes on to say that his girlfriend's sister worked the same day as Patsy. He states that Gene came to Patsy's work and showed her the newspaper with the marriage license in it and Patsy left the nursing home. This confirms what I believed that Larry knew that his brother Gene was going to kill Patsy. Why else would he run around town and go almost directly to the police? Why wouldn't he go straight to Gene's house which was right there in town a couple of blocks from him? Was he trying to find them to stop it? Did he see Gene and Debra with Patsy when he was out? Perhaps he was in on the planning and then had second thoughts. He frantically went to police three times that day to get help without turning his brother in of what he suspected was going to happen. Or, was he involved in it and needed to look like the "concerned ex-husband?" But why didn't he get the police to go to Gene's with him? There is more to this story. Did he ever tell police that Gene threatened Patsy or again, was he setting up an alibi? Just to be certain, I needed to know what Patsy knew about Larry's relationship with Shirley.

Cummins: "So your wife was aware that you were with this other woman and had kids with her?"
Calloway: "<u>Yeah, yeah, I mean… that's one reason we got divorced</u>."

I already knew that Patsy was aware of the affair. Given the chance again, I would ask him, "What kind of deal did you make with Patsy to keep her quiet about the arson. Is that why you deeded the property over to her when she filed?"

Cummins: "Ok, because you were seeing both of them at the same time and got her pregnant. Yeah, I get it. You were having an affair."
Calloway: "<u>Yeah</u>."

The "other" reason he got divorced is because he burned down Patsy's house for the insurance money. Patsy was aware of the affairs and of the second pregnancy. Larry wasn't afraid she just walked off mad or he wouldn't have desperately tried to get help from the police. He was afraid Gene was going to kill her over the arson deal or again, he needed an alibi. I follow up with that.

Cummins: "So the story that Darrell gives me is that Gene, went to her work that day and that was verified by a witness… and Gene… he picked her up."
Calloway: "<u>Well, you know… that's Shirley's sister. The one that came to the apartment and told me and her.</u>"
Cummins: "What's her name?"
Calloway: "<u>Uh, "Maryanne</u>."
Cummins: "She came to Shirley's apartment, your's

and Shirley's apartment?"

Calloway: "<u>Exactly. Riverbend apartments. And told us that Patsy had left work, and Vernon (Gene) had showed her a newspaper. The newspaper had in there where I had applied for a marriage license</u>."

Cummins: "And… she saw the paper?"

Calloway: "<u>He showed it to her, from my understanding</u>."

Cummins: "I'm not trying to berate your affair or anything, but were you still sleeping with both women?"

Calloway: "Yes I was."

For me the answers are clear. Gene Calloway threatened Larry and Patsy over the arson. Larry was aware of Gene's plan to kill her or he believed wholeheartedly that Gene would make good on his threat to slice her throat from ear to ear. So why would police continue to look at him as a person of interest or possible suspect? Perhaps because he failed his polygraph. I'm sure the detective had the same questions in his mind that I had. Was Larry being truthful or setting up an alibi? Why didn't he go directly to Gene's house to stop it, instead of going to the police? What did he tell police that first day about Patsy's disappearance? Why did he tell them he was there? Police should've asked him these questions.

Cummins: "Our goal at Missing Persons News is to find missing people."

Calloway: "<u>And that's the main thing I want</u>."

According to speech analysis, it is clear that he not only wants Patsy found, but wants his name cleared. That's why he uses the word "main" in that statement. Did the brothers set up Patsy's murder so the police would have to choose between two suspects?

Cummins: "Do you have any idea where Gene may have put Patsy?"
Calloway: "Every place that I can think of, that he knows, I have walked and looked. Like I said, I have searched and searched and searched."

This direct statement indicates that he has a good idea that Patsy was killed at the hands of his brother, even though he won't admit to it. This again contradicts his earlier statement that he had no idea of what happened to Patsy. In regard to Patsy's remains, Larry says, "that he knows." That wasn't a generalized statement about a missing person, rather he refers to his brother Gene and places Gene knows of. Why would he search places Gene knows of if he didn't know he killed Patsy? He heard his brother Jimmy speak of seeing her body first-hand and yet he still speaks of Patsy in future tense. This again reiterates that he didn't kill her, but he surely knew about it in advance. To get an idea of what Gene did to Patsy and what role Debra played in her murder, I press further.

Cummins: "Do you remember what kind of vehicle he was driving back then?"
Calloway: "He had a Blazer, a black blazer."
Cummins: "Where did your brother Jimmy tell you and Darrell that he saw the body at, in the back of the truck?"
Calloway: "That was down at Hunter's trailer court. That's where Gene lived, my mom lived."
Cummins: "So he said he saw it at Hunter's trailer court?"

Calloway: "<u>Yeah</u>."

Jimmy Calloway saw the body of Patsy in the back of the truck at Hunter's Trailer Court, which was only blocks, from Patsy's work. Or did he? Was he the person I was seeing in the car in my visuals or was it Larry. I don't know what Jimmy looked like back then. If Gene killed Patsy out on 1414 at her trailer, it would've been a bold move to drive back to town with a dead body in his truck. It's not likely that Gene would risk bringing Patsy's remains all the way back into town. So the blood in Patsy's trailer belongs to whom? Who died out there? Is that why Larry is so terrified of his brother? In my visuals I saw Patsy inside her trailer getting her throat cut. Was my mind in the wrong trailer or was it someone else I was seeing. I still suspect Gene as a serial killer and this is potential confirmation of that. I believe the police need to do a DNA profile on the blood in the trailer to determine whether or not it's Patsy's. What if Jimmy lied? Was he with Gene the day Patsy was murdered? Was Debra there too? In my visuals, I saw Gene in the trailer killing Patsy, and a red head and another man in the white car outside.

Cummins: "So he said he saw it at Hunter's trailer court?"
Calloway: "<u>Yeah</u>."
Cummins: "Where Gene lived?"
Calloway: "Yeah. See mom owned his house and lived two or three trailers down from him. "
Cummins: "What about your sister Mildred. Supposedly, she saw Debra walking down the street in this wig and uniform and coat. Then she pulls up and it's not Patsy, it's Debra?"

Calloway: "I had talked to her about that. She cannot remember exactly 'cause she's 79-years-old. She's got mind and heart trouble and all this."

In his statement he said, "She cannot remember exactly." Using the word exactly in this context means that she does remember partially and he slipped with his statement admitting it. This again goes to show that he believes she was murdered at the hands of his brother and refuses to come forward with the truth and the family is covering for their brother Gene. It also contradicts his earlier statement about not speaking to Mildred when Patsy first went missing. I'm certain now that Mildred is one of the "them" he was referring to when he says "she was supposedly seen walking."

Cummins: "We're trying to get coordinates for where her remains might be so Darrell can bury her. That's what our goal is and our interest. The main goal of what we do, is just to find their location and there's nowhere that you can think of, where he might have put Patsy? I heard that Gene made a statement that she's right under his nose."

Now my "tells" are showing. When I said main goal, I almost scared him off because he now knows I have more than one and the other goal is for justice. When I use the word just in that context, it's a direct indication of deceit. After realizing my slip up, I switched gears so he would focus on Gene.

Calloway: "I've heard that talk too. It's just words, cause I've heard a thousand different stories, and… I don't know."

Cummins: "You don't have any idea where he might have put her?"
Calloway: "<u>I have searched everywhere that I can think of that he has been. I have walked and walked and walked</u>."

If he didn't have reason to believe Gene killed Patsy, he wouldn't search everywhere that Gene had been. Has Larry witnessed Gene kill before? Remember, he's again referring to searching where Gene had walked. He'd only heard Jimmy tell him about seeing the body of Patsy, several days prior to our interview, according to him. I'm just not buying into it. I'm certain he didn't search the whole county in a couple of days.

Who died in Patsy's trailer? Was it Patsy or someone else? If it's Patsy, then Larry had to know about the blood. The floor underneath where the carpet had been was saturated. The floor underneath the linoleum was saturated as well and there was a noticeable blood stain on the bathroom door. Bear the dog made a positive hit for a cadaver. I believe Gene killed someone prior to killing Patsy and after. Maybe this is another reason why Larry was afraid of Gene. One of those killings may have occurred in that trailer. When I get the feeling that someone is a serial killer, I can't shake it. If I go by statement analysis, Larry would've had to have seen the blood in the trailer where he lived with Patsy. Maybe it's not her blood and she was killed, perhaps in Gene's truck. I needed more information.

Chapter Nine: Blood is in the Trailer

Cummins: "What about the trailer? Did anything ever happen at the trailer? Why does he (Darrell) keep insisting that the cops search the trailer? They had search teams out there and they didn't recover her body."

Calloway: "Well see, now, <u>when I was working with Violet, we brought a cadaver dog in and searched somewhere. I don't remember where it was. But it was somewhere out there near the trailer, out in that part of the country I think</u>."

Cummins: "You didn't find anything?"

Calloway: "<u>No</u>."

I noticed that Larry says they searched "near the trailer, but not in it. Why would he have them bring a dog out there and not search his trailer, if anything, to clear his name? If he knew there was blood in the trailer, he'd have avoided that area at all cost. Then he said "out near the trailer." Was this another missed opportunity by police? He said they searched, "somewhere." This was direct avoidance of the question at hand, indicating he's hiding the truth.

Cummins: "Did the dog hit on anything?"

Calloway: "<u>Nope. And now they've built a whole bunch of houses back in there</u>."

Cummins: "Is that where she lived before… where you and her lived before?"

Calloway: "<u>Yep. She lived out on 1414</u>."

First Larry says he doesn't remember where they searched, then he says they built a whole bunch of houses back in there. But if Larry was truly working with police and they brought in a cadaver dog when she went missing, he should've had them search the trailer. It also contradicts his statement that police only searched the cars and not her trailer, because they were searching back behind her property. Maybe Cadaver dogs aren't always right, but with the blood evidence in that trailer, I suspect Bear did his job well because there was a lot of blood in the pictures I'd seen.

The trailer hadn't been scrubbed down to each crevice, but it took luminal to show where it had been cleaned up. Did Larry witness someone die at the hands of his brother before that, or is that Patsy's blood in her home? Larry isn't going to accompany officers to the trailer with a cadaver dog in tow if he knows someone was killed in there. This strengthens my wish for law enforcement to collect DNA samples from the trailer to see if they can identify the victim. Only the killers know when that killing took place. If Patsy was killed inside the trailer, no way did he "not" know about it. He was at Shirley's in the afternoon and said he was waiting at home for Patsy that evening. Did he go there and help clean it up?

Cummins: "Ok, so you were living with your ex-wife and you were living with your girlfriend at the same time?"
Calloway: "No. No. I wasn't living with the girlfriend."
Cummins: "Oh, but you said you were in Shirley's apartment, so you were just kind of staying there?"
Calloway: "It was her apartment."
Cummins: "Oh, it was Shirley's apartment. It wasn't your apartment."
Calloway: "Exactly."
Cummins: "Is there anything you want to add Larry?"
Calloway: "Not that I can think of. Only that I'd really like to find her body. You know, I've thought about this since then. It's, people don't understand what you go

through until you go through it."

This statement from Larry clearly indicates that he believes Patsy is deceased and he wants to find her and exonerate himself. It is also very narcissistic in nature. He's concerned with what he's gone through and not at all concerned about what Patsy went through. In a prior statement, Larry confirmed with the word "exactly" when questioned about him living with Shirley. His two stories are conflicting, but both indicate that he wants to find Patsy. It's still not clear if he helped plan it or not. Now, onto the question of if he failed the lie detector.

Chapter Ten: Failing the Polygraph

Cummins: "Did they tell you why you failed the polygraph?"
Calloway: "<u>Because I was thinking about her and where she could be and what happened to her… is she alright. You know</u>. The only thing you can answer when they give you a polygraph is straight yes or no. You can't have nothing on your mind. They wanted me to take another one. I have <u>Parkinson</u>'s. You know, the shaking disease. I went over there to take another one a year… a year or two ago. But with my shaking, uh, the guy who gives it to ya, would not give it to me. Because of that… he said it would affect it."

At the time of the polygraph, I believe Larry failed because he knew his brother killed Patsy. I believe he discussed it with his sister who saw Debra that day and she refused to speak of it to protect her brother Gene and perhaps her own safety. This left Larry out on a limb and further set him up as the "bad guy" in the eyes of the police. They didn't know why he failed the test, only that he failed it. He was Patsy's ex-husband. He was getting re-married to another young woman. Gene did a fabulous job at setting his brother up for the murder, or perhaps that was the plan in the first place. That makes it difficult for police to determine which one is guilty or if both are guilty. This was Darrell Kessinger's question. I don't think the initial failure of the polygraph examination had anything to do with Parkinson's disease. As an older male with Parkinson's, the examiner was right to refuse the test some fifteen years later.

Cummins: It might show up as a lie when you're not actually lying."
Calloway: "Yeah. It's a machine. And… Me and detective Whittaker got into it over there, because of that. He said I didn't want to take it. I says I that I'm not… I'm here to take it! I said, "You go in there and tell them to give it to me." And he would not do it."
Cummins: "So what about your brother Gene. Is he older or younger than you?"
Calloway: "He's what… 69."
Cummins: "And he passed his polygraph?"
Calloway: "That's what everybody tells me."
Cummins: "But you don't know if that's true?"
Calloway: "No, I don't. I can't confirm."
Cummins: "But Jimmy passed all three of his."

Police confirm that Jimmy passed his polygraphs. Did they ever ask Jimmy if he was at Patsy's trailer with Gene and Debra? That I can't answer.

Calloway: "So I've heard. Now, I don't know. I wasn't there. I've read that in the paper."

Cummins: "Now, Jimmy said he had her in the back of the truck. Did he say where he took her to after that? Or did he confront your brother?"

Calloway: "<u>See the first time I heard about what Jimmy told Darrell, was with Darrell down there</u>."

Notice that Larry avoided my direct question in regard to Patsy's remains. If that's the first time he heard about what Jimmy told Darrell about seeing Patsy's body, why did he search everywhere that Gene knew, unless he knew or suspected Gene killed her? He also refrained from commenting on whether or not Jimmy described where Gene took Patsy's remains. He also lied about speaking to his sister Mildred that day. He disassociated himself from his own daughter Tanya. I specifically asked Larry if Jimmy had confronted Gene and he avoided the question. Why?

Cummins: "That was the first time you'd ever heard about it?"

Calloway: "<u>The details that Jimmy gave to Darrell</u>."

Cummins: "Ok. And that was when? When did that take place?"

Calloway: "<u>Um… a month or so ago. Jimmy told them years ago</u>."

Cummins: "Jimmy told the police what happened years ago?… back when she went missing?"

Calloway: "<u>Not when she went missing</u>… well, he turned it in to police… of what he knew… when she was missing… and they were searching… and <u>they didn't do nothing about it. Then when he come up on another charge, and we asked him… I was with him at the lawyers, and he told some details that I heard from him</u>. And then, when we met with Darrell, me and him, cause Jimmy turned state's evidence, see. So. Um.

When me and Jimmy met with Darrell down in town, and they was talkin, Darrell was asking him about it and stuff, that's when I heard the other details I didn't know about."

At this point, Larry realizes the mistake he'd just made with me and tries to cover it up. He admits that it wasn't the first time he'd heard about Jimmy seeing Patsy's body in Gene's truck. Another direct lie comes out of his mouth. Shocking! He goes on to reveal that he'd heard about it a few years ago when his brother Jimmy got in trouble. That still doesn't account for early on when he searched everywhere that Gene went and knew of. He also said that Jimmy told police right after Patsy went missing. It doesn't answer why he went to police immediately, but I already knew why and it was confirmed, so he couldn't hide the lies any longer. Larry needed an alibi for that day so he could exonerate himself in regard to Patsy's murder.

Cummins: "Did Jimmy say anything of where he took her or put her? He never confronted Gene?"
Calloway: "He didn't know. He told me and Darrell, he did not know."
Cummins: "He didn't confront Gene about it?"
Calloway: "I can't remember that. I just can't remember. I told him no. See, I wasn't with him when he was around Gene that day."

I'd heard first hand from Darrell Kessinger that Jimmy gave him directions to where Gene put Patsy's remains. When I asked Larry if Jimmy confronted Gene about seeing the body and Patsy's murder, Larry first says, "I can't remember that. I just can't remember." Then he says, "**I told him no.**" And now the truth **SLIPS out!**

Larry Calloway went to the police frantically because Jimmy told him he saw Patsy's body on the day she went missing! He told him NO! In other words, DON'T CONFRONT GENE! He knew the very first day that Gene had killed Patsy! Larry goes on to say, "See, I wasn't with him when he was around Gene that day." Why would he make that statement? Was this to try and disassociate himself with the murder? I expect this was the case. This confirmed my suspicion that he knew Gene killed Patsy! He then goes almost directly to the police. Was it to keep an eye on the police and keep them distracted? He knew that Gene planned to kill her or else he wouldn't have gone to police UNLESS it was to establish an alibi.

Larry realized that he slipped up and let it out by saying, "I told him no." There is no other possible reason he would tell his brother not to confront Gene Calloway about seeing Patsy's body, if he didn't know about it. So Jimmy had to tell him THAT day. But then Larry tries to cover it up and says that he wasn't with Jimmy that day. Where was he? Was he at Patsy's trailer, sitting in the car when she was murdered? He had to have spoken with Jimmy, perhaps on the phone. The light went on for me and now I had the truth. I still wanted further confirmation, so I continued the interview. I wanted his feelings about his fear of Gene. I wanted to know if he was protecting Gene or was he terrified of him. Or was he trying to keep Gene from killing Jimmy and his own girlfriend and current wife Shirley? Either way, this is another member of the Calloway family that obstructed justice. The question is, "WHY?"

Chapter Eleven: Fear of a Killer

Now Larry slipped and admitted that Jimmy told him of seeing Patsy's body on the day she disappeared, but in an inadvertent manner. I wanted to know why in the hell he wouldn't tell police of such a thing. Would he cover up for his brother who set him up? This was an intensely planned out murder. They went so far as to purchase a wig, nurse's uniform and coat to look like Patsy's. She was murdered on the anniversary of her filing for divorce. Gene wouldn't have made a threat to Larry and Shirley that they're all going down, unless he had something to do with the planning. Perhaps Gene had something else on him that would be revealed later. Moving on…

Cummins: "Were you guys intimidated by your brother Gene?"
Calloway: "<u>I'm not. I ain't scared of nobody walking</u>."

Interesting that when Larry replies to my question, he uses the present tense in his statements, but avoids the past tense in regard to fear of his brother Gene.

Cummins: "Was Jimmy?"
Calloway: "<u>Well, he's scared of him</u>. Yeah. Like I said, you know, he's a little challenged there."
Cummins: "Darrell told me that Gene had threatened you and Shirley. Is that true?"
Calloway: "<u>He has</u>… <u>he has never threatened me. If he's threatened her, it's been that I'm unaware. Cause he has never threatened me. Cause he knows I'd take it straight to his face</u>."
(I asked Darrell Kessinger about this. Darrell claims that during their meeting in Hartford, According to

Kessinger, Shirley confirmed that Gene had threatened her and Larry.) In a later interview, Shirley claims that Gene had threatened them on several occasions.

First, Larry says, "He has," but then he pauses and continues to say Gene hasn't threatened him and he's unaware if he's threatened his wife. So he starts this statement saying his brother had threatened him, but then changes it. When I interviewed Shirley Calloway, she also confirmed that Gene had threatened them both. It was obvious to me that Larry was terrified of his older brother Gene, but what did that terror entail? What else did Gene do that Larry is so terrified of? It couldn't have been the murder of Patsy unless Larry witnessed it. There is still the probability that Larry needed an alibi. Pressing on...

Cummins: "So Darrell's not telling the truth about that?"
Calloway: "No. No he's not."
Cummins: "Darrell's trying to insinuate that Gene threatened to kill you and Shirley, if you opened your mouths or if you said anything, and you're saying that's not true?"
Calloway: "For 19 years, I've been trying to find what happened. And if I knew the truth, I would tell the truth."

As a reader, you can't hear the determination and inflection in Larry's prior statement. He was very upset and stern when he said if he knew the truth, he'd tell the truth, almost to the point of anger in that he hasn't been heard or that I wasn't buying his lies.

Cummins: "And he's never threatened you over it."
Calloway: "<u>He has never threatened me of anything. I've already said this before. I don't back off from him</u>."

Larry says that Darrell is lying, yet he states, "For 19 years, I've been trying to find what happened. And if I knew the truth, I would tell the truth." Now, we already know that's a lie. Jimmy told him he'd seen the body of Patsy the day she died. I believe that his ego has taken over and he doesn't want to appear weak. I believe he's hiding many secrets, but the main secret is whether or not he was involved in the planning of Patsy's murder. I also believe he's terrified of Gene and perhaps guilt played a role in his answer which is why he says, "For 19 years, I've been trying to find what happened." This makes perfect sense, so I continue the line of questions.

Cummins: "So is Gene bigger than you or smaller than you?"
Calloway: "<u>Oh, He's a lot bigger than I am. He weighs 300 and something pounds now. He's about 6' and I'm 5'4</u>."
Cummins: "Has Gene ever been to jail, other than for the arson?"
Calloway: "<u>Oh yeah</u>."
Cummins: Tanya's your daughter? And Angie's the one who's got the rings?"
Calloway: "Now, I don't know that about the jewelry."

I find it interesting that when I ask him about his daughter Tanya again, he avoids answering that particular question. Again, he distances himself from his daughter. Instead, he focuses on the missing wedding rings.

Cummins: "Well, a statement was made on Topix that she had the rings, and I'm just wondering how she got them."
Calloway: "Well, she had a bunch of rings, different rings and stuff."
Cummins: "But not her wedding rings?" (Patsy's wedding rings from her marriage to Larry)
Calloway: "That, I'd have to ask her. That's just something I heard. I don't know. I couldn't tell you. See I had… when Patsy disappeared I stayed out there for a while with the phones on. To keep the phones, you know… in case somebody called… something."

When asked about the rings, his mind takes him back out to Patsy's house. He said he'd heard about Angie having the rings. But why take your mind from the rings to Patsy's house? Was he there when she was murdered? Did they take the rings off of Patsy and keep them for Gene's daughter-in-law Angie? Who knows. Is he trying to back-track to cover up the lie he told me about going to the police because Patsy didn't come home? At this point, Larry is attempting to plot his course again.

Cummins: "You stayed out where? At the trailer? Or at Shirley's?"
Calloway: "At the trailer. And the detective Ballard, had me move town for fear of my life."

There you have it folks. He moved town for fear of his life. All the while, he needs to exonerate himself of the murder because Gene had him practically hemmed up if they ever found Patsy. The first person police usually look at is the husband or ex-husband. There are obvious reasons for that. The police also ignored Jimmy Calloway when he reported to them that he saw her body. Without a body, how could he prove that Gene killed Patsy? If Patsy's body was found, Gene could've said Larry did it and Shirley was just covering for him. Larry could've said Gene did it and this leaves the police to figure out who is lying. Was there a murder pact among the three of them? It's probable. There is all kinds of blood in that trailer and I'd like to know Larry's whereabouts on that day. Did he have a life insurance policy on Patsy? I still get Gene in my mind as a predator and sexual deviant so I pursue this line of questioning to Larry. I also get Larry as a pedophile. After speaking with Shirley, I learned she got pregnant when she was a teen and Larry was in his late 30s. So far, I'm right on track. That still doesn't answer the question of who's blood is all over that trailer. If it's Patsy's blood, Larry had to know about it. Why else was he afraid of Gene?

Chapter Twelve: Back to the Trailer

Cummins: "So I'm just curious. All of this blood and everything in the bathroom that was all over the trailer. Where did that come from?"
Calloway: "Huh? There was no blood in the trailer. What?"
Cummins: "They had a criminologist go in the trailer and spray the trailer down with luminal, and there's blood all over the hall and the bathroom and the wall, and in the floor. You don't know where that came from?"
Calloway: "No I don't. You see, somebody else lived

there before. I thought it was them other people."

How could Larry think it was them other people if he didn't see blood in the trailer? Was he just deflecting because he felt defensive or did he actually see something that happened out there and possibly partake in it? Back to the alibi theory.

Cummins: "I don't know what a DNA has determined, but they sent a cadaver dog there in the bathroom, and the cadaver dog went in there and sat down. Then, they had someone go in and spray it down with luminal, and there was blood on the walls and the ceiling and the bathroom, and the floor outside the door, but you don't know where that blood came from?"

Calloway: "I've never seen any blood in there. Never."

Cummins: "So you don't think it's Patricia's blood?"

Calloway: "I couldn't tell you either way. I don't know. But, I've never seen blood in there."

Cummins: "If you're living there with her, and that's Patricia's blood, doesn't that make it look like you're the one that killed her?"

Calloway: "Well, yeah, I look guilty. But uh, there was no blood. I can't say who's it was, but…"

Cummins: "There was no blood in the trailer at the time?"

Calloway: "Now, I didn't go back out to the trailer after she come up missing. I went looking. I went out there, nobody was out there. I left, and went looking for her."

Cummins: "Yeah, but just a minute ago, you said you sat there and waited for her."

Calloway: "No, that was that night."

So I've already caught him in one lie. I know he's seen blood in there, because he couldn't have believed it was "them other people" if he didn't see it. It concerns me when he says, "<u>I can't say who's it was, but…</u>" He stops himself from completing that sentence because he knows he's revealing too much information. He also used the word "WAS" meaning past tense. If he said, "I can't say who's blood it is, that would mean that he either didn't know the person and that the person is still with us in the present sense. He uses "was" in the past tense, meaning that person is no longer with us. It also takes him to a place of recall in his mind. He knows the blood is still in the trailer so this is the only explanation. Then Larry states, "Now, I didn't go back out to the trailer after she come up missing. I went looking. I went out there, nobody was out there. I left, and went looking for her." Earlier in our interview, Larry claims he stayed out there for a while after she went missing. Which is it? At this point, he's covering his tracks because he knows he's just been busted. When he says the word "later," how much later is he referring to? Is it that night; is it a month; a year; two years? In my opinion, Larry probably was a witness to the crime that occurred in Patsy's trailer, perhaps even a participant. I continue to see if Gene was at the trailer that night.

Cummins: "Is there any way Gene could've been in your trailer? If you found the keys at 5:00 is there any way that Vernon Gene…"
Calloway: "<u>I can confirm that, because Patsy had the keys to the trailer.</u>"

Larry says, "I can confirm that." How can he confirm that Gene was in the trailer? How did he know Gene had Patsy's keys? He's trying to come up with answers because he now knows that the blood has been found. If he didn't know Patsy was murdered by Gene, then there is no way he could "confirm" anything unless he saw Gene with the keys at the trailer. We already know that he lied about not knowing what happened to Patsy. Again, what is he hiding? He is inadvertently pointing the finger to his brother Gene again. In order to see Gene with those keys, he had to be there.

This conversation was about the blood in the trailer and the possibility that Gene was in the trailer that day or night. Unless he saw him there with the keys that day or night, there is no way he could confirm anything. Larry referred to the person in that trailer in the past tense, we can deduce that he saw Gene in the trailer at the same time as the blood and the victim, Patsy. I question him about the keys again.

Cummins: "But the keys were found in the car by you?"

Calloway: "Right. They were in the floor, underneath. The seat was not up where it's normally, with her driving, 'cause she always had the seat all the way up. I wouldn't have been able to get in with the seat up. When I got in, the seat was skooched back. I looked in the ignition. I didn't really pay attention to the floor because it was dark. I looked. Did not see it. So when I went back to the police station and talked to 'em, they said, you know, I was told to look around for keys. And when I went back, I had to use my lighter. I found the keys, and I took it over there like they'd asked me."

Larry just stated that he could "confirm" that Gene had the keys, but then he said he found the keys in the car. It can't be both. I noticed that he said he got "into" the car. He goes on to say that the seat was skooched back. Why would he sit in this car to drive it, if he didn't have the keys? Was he pretending to look for the keys for the benefit of fooling the police?

Cummins: "So, if that's Patsy's blood, somebody had to have been in there to clean that blood up."
Calloway: "<u>That's what I say, and I just don't see how they could do it that quick</u>."

When I ask him in regard to the blood and clean up, he uses the word, "they." He said, "That's what I'd say and I just don't see how <u>they</u> could do it that quick." Who is the "<u>they</u>" he's referring to? He didn't say him or her, he said "they." If he only suspected his brother Gene, he would've used the word "he," not "they." This could go to memory recall.

Cummins: "If you were living in that trailer with Patsy and she was killed there, how did the blood get cleaned up?"

Calloway: "<u>That's exactly what I don't know. I'm just not believing that, that's what it is</u>. When me and Darrell was talking, I told him where that trailer sit. I said, "Has anybody ever checked that trailer? I said, "It's sitting up there towards Dundee.""

The word "exactly" is also used out of context if he didn't know. If he didn't know, he would not use the word "exactly" in that statement. He would've said, "I don't know," or "I have no idea." Exactly indicates that that's "exactly" or "precisely" what it is. He knows, because he was there.

When Larry says, "I'm just not believing that that's what it is," he uses the word "just" again, out of context. This also indicates deceit. In other words, "He's just believing that that's what it is," because he knows it's Patsy's blood. He was there or he couldn't confirm anything about Gene having the keys. He wouldn't know about the rings. He wouldn't try to make himself look innocent by going all over the place handing out flyers. He wouldn't have gone to police that day if he was just expecting Patsy to be angry.

Cummins: "So you told Darrell to check the trailer?"
Calloway: "Yeah, <u>I'm the one who told Darrell where the trailer and stuff was. I told him that they'd never checked it, that I knew of</u>."

If Larry had already been out there with Violet and an officer with a cadaver dog, why would he beg Darrell to go out there and search it again? Maybe he was trying to throw Darrell a bone. I believe Larry is lying, to try and get the finger off of himself.

Darrell Kessinger tells me that this was a bold-faced lie by Larry. He said he inquired about Patsy's trailer to other people, not Larry. He said he was the one who mentioned it to Larry, not the other way around. This makes the most sense to me, because Larry knows there is blood in that trailer. Since we know he took a cadaver dog out there with police after Patsy's murder, but they never searched it, maybe this last statement was his way of thumbing his nose to Darrell.

Chapter Thirteen: How Far Does it Go

Cummins: "Was your brother Gene working for Phillip Ballard as a farm-hand?"

(Phillip Ballard was the original investigator on the Patsy Kessinger Calloway case.)

Calloway: "No. No no no. Now, we had a cuttin crew… of tobacco, back in the early '80s. And we went around this town cuttin tobacco for people. Ballard found out we was a cuttin crew, and he hired us. Because of his tobacco, and his brother-in-law was a state trooper named Jerry, he helped us. But there was 5 or 6 of us anyway."
Cummins: "So you and your brother worked on a cutting crew out there, just hanging tobacco, cutting it, pressing it?"
Calloway: "Yeah, Yeah. We done that for people all around this county yeah. That was on our spare time, because I worked for the forestry at the time, too."

Larry Calloway confirms the graphic detail in which his brother Jimmy Calloway, describes having seen Patsy's body. He said he'd warned his ex-wife Patsy on many occasions not to ever get in a vehicle with Vernon Gene. He said that Gene wanted Patsy and that Patsy did not like Gene. Larry says that he was in love with both women at the time and he didn't know what to do because Shirley was pregnant again. When Patsy went missing, his second child with Shirley had already been born. Does this go to recall? Did he need someone to take care of the problem? He'd hired Gene to burn down the house. Maybe he hired him to kill Patsy. My question about Gene Calloway is still the same. Is he in fact a serial killer? Why would Larry "warn" Patsy of anything about his brother if he didn't fear him or if no threats were made? He wouldn't.

Larry Calloway goes on to state that Patsy knew about the arson, because she was in on his plans. Kessinger claims that Larry and his sister were separated at the time and this was not true. Darrell Kessinger says his sister warned Larry Calloway on several occasions not to burn down her house. This statement by Darrell could only be true if Patsy was aware they had a plan to do the arson. Larry Calloway continues stating that, "Gene knows places." He states that he's been searching for his ex-wife for nineteen years, and that he was in love with her at the time of her disappearance. When asked by me outright, "Did you kill Patsy Calloway or help plan her murder?" Larry Calloway replies, "No. Absolutely not." He denies any wrong doing in regard to the disappearance of his ex-wife or knowledge thereof. Larry Calloway goes on to admit other factors that Darrell Kessinger spoke of, including that his brother Jimmy is on trial and turning states evidence.

It's interesting to me that when I asked Larry if he killed or was in on the planning to kill Patsy, he didn't say, "What plan?" "There was no plan." Instead he said, "No. Absolutely not." He also didn't deny there was a plan to kill Patsy.

Getting back to my original thoughts regarding the perpetrators, I told Darrell Kessinger in my raw reading that I felt Patsy's case was like the "Hooker" case. For those of you not familiar, a kidnapped woman was kept in a wooden box, under a bed. She was repeatedly raped and tortured at the hands of the husband and his wife in ordeals that are too horrific to describe. She was their sex slave and punching bag. The wife helped to facilitate the crimes against the victim. I felt like Gene Calloway wanted Patsy sexually and it was more than just killing her to cover up for the arson. I felt/feel like Gene and Debra Calloway were sexual predators that raped, dominated women, and killed them. I suspect Gene of killing two men as well. I have no proof of any of that, it is just what I feel in my inner most thoughts. When I look at Debra, my "gadar" goes off. I believe she was bisexual, if not a lesbian. I have no problem with someone being gay, unless it involves the crimes I'm accusing her of, like the disappearance of Patsy Calloway.

Larry Calloway stated to me that "Gene wanted Patsy and Patsy did not like Gene." In other portions of our taped interview, Larry's wife Shirley goes on to tell me that she was afraid of Gene and that he'd made sexual advances toward her in the past. She describes a moment where she was standing in her yard and Gene was there and approached her. She said she went into the house and stayed away from him. She said when Gene was around the, hair on the back of her neck would stand up.

Shirley Calloway (Larry's current wife) told me that Gene came to her apartment once and she was alone. She said he always had a crazy look in his eyes. She said he made advances toward her that day, and the phone rang. She said when she answered the phone she forced the person to stay on the other line, so Gene would know that if he did something to her, she could get help. She said although the other party hung up the phone, she pretended to still talk until Gene left her apartment. This was shortly after Patsy went missing. She said she noticed a large bite mark on Gene's right hand. She told me that Gene was left-handed and there was a very visible, purple bruise, in the shape of a bite mark on his right hand.

I asked Darrell Kessinger about the bite mark. He said that Detective Phillip Ballard set up meetings with him and family to discuss Patsy's case. He said that somehow, Gene Calloway would show up at every meeting. At one of those meetings, Darrell said he saw the bite mark on Gene's hand and confronted him about it. Darrell told me that his sister Theresa Kassinger and her husband Dustin were at that particular meeting. Darrell said that Dustin asked the detective, "Who is this Vernon Calloway? I heard he was over there that day." At that moment, Vernon Gene who was standing behind them said, "I am Vernon Calloway and I have a wife, and a girlfriend working there, and it's none of your fucking business." That's when Darrell jumped up off the counter and got in Gene's face and said, "If you had anything to do with the disappearance of Patsy, then THAT's my business!" He noticed the bite mark immediately on Gene's right had between the thumb and forefinger, because he had that hand up above his head, leaning against the wall.

Darrell said he got in Gene Calloway's face and was screaming at him, "You've got a bite mark right there on your hand! Where did it come from? What did you do to my sister?" Darrell said Detective Ballard made Gene Calloway leave. He said he asked Detective Ballard why he didn't arrest Gene.

After Gene left, according to Darrell, Detective Ballard asked him, "Why do you think Gene's showing up to these meetings?" Darrell replied to the detective, "You're the detective, why don't you tell me? I'll tell you why he's here. He's here to cover his own tracks and make sure we're not onto him! You give me two weeks to cover up my tracks and I'll come here and commit any crime you want me to." According to Darrell, Detective Ballard replied, "I'm not gonna have you come down and criticize the way I handle an investigation. I'll lock you up!" Darrell said at that moment, he knew that Gene had done something to Patsy because it was a clear bruised bite mark on his hand and it was deep. He said he also felt like justice would never see the light of day. But why did the detective threaten Darrell and not Gene? Again, why wasn't Gene arrested? There has to be a reason. Why didn't the police go looking for Patsy for 20 days? Why didn't they search Patsy's trailer. One can only speculate about this.

At this point, I had enough information that was confirmed and recorded by me to release my article about Patsy. When asking questions in regard to an arrest, I say this realizing it is extremely difficult to put on a murder trial when you have people covering up and lying for someone. It makes it even tougher when you have no body and someone who is set up to look like the murderer who didn't actually do it, but probably participated in the planning. Back in the beginning, many errors were made. In 2012, Patsy's case was 19-years-old at the time. It was a daunting task for police officials and the prosecutor who came into the investigation long after the murder occurred. Nineteen years earlier, it's kind of easy to see why they didn't pursue charges. They had no body and the only evidence sought out was the word of a man who may have been involved in the killing. Hell, they didn't even leave their desks to go find Patsy's car when she went missing. They had Larry do it. Duh!

If you're wondering about the trailer as I am, Darrell Kesssinger told me Chris Williams from the JPRST spoke to Judge Renona Browning. Kessinger claims that Judge Browning said she would sign off on a warrant for Patsy's trailer. I confirmed this with Judge Browning. At the time Darrell and the search teams checked out Patsy's trailer, Darrell said he also spoke with the prosecutor, Tim Coleman and the prosecutor didn't want to pursue searching the trailer in this case. I'm certain at this point, the police already knew what had happened to Patsy, but why hadn't the suspects been arrested? They had an eye-witness. Patsy's case had changed hands many times over 19 years. With the witnesses and family members being tight-lipped about the murder, it was a most difficult case to present to a jury. The family would have to come out with what they knew.

Chapter Fourteen: The Arrests

I published my original article, "**An Arson, A Wig, and A Murder, No Justice for Patsy Calloway,**" on September 27th, 2012. Since then, new facts have come to light. Almost three weeks after I published that article about Patsy's disappearance, arrests were made. I don't know what, if anything, my article release had to do with the arrests of Debra and Vernon Gene Calloway, but I suspect it had something to do with it. I knew publishing it would shake the family members into telling what they knew and it could only get us one step closer to finding Patsy. After all, the public now knew there is an eye-witness to seeing Patsy's body.

Putting it out to the public that blood was found in the trailer and posting those images, along with the acknowledgement of Jimmy seeing Patsy's body, let the public know this case was solvable. I don't want the public to distrust the police, because not all cops are bad cops. I'm certain Bryan Whittaker is a fabulous detective and he did what he had to do to push this case forward. I can't say the same thing about some others.

According to speech analysis, Larry probably helped plan the murder of his live-in, ex-wife. The rules of speech show that Larry almost certainly knew it was going to happen. I know that the photos of the blood in the trailer were very graphic in the article I wrote, but it made sense to put it in there, because I knew people would crawl out of the woodwork to clear themselves. I'm sure in my mind that Detective Whittaker knew what I was up to. I told Darrell of my plans. He agreed to go along with it because this was about finding his sister. If you're going to catch a killer or killers, sometimes you have to be deceitful. I needed to shake the branches to get the apples to fall off the tree. It wasn't about tricking the public or making the police look stupid. Police have to follow the rules of evidence and law. I know that. From my perspective, this was about finding justice for Patsy and hoping to recover her remains. The following is a portion of the article I wrote the day after the suspects were arrested:

Hartford KY (MPN) — Today, two arrests were made in the murder of Patricia Ann Calloway, who disappeared on March 3, 1993. According to a press release by Kentucky State Police Public Affairs officer Corey King, the following summary was given: The Kentucky State Police has charged two with the murder of Patricia Calloway.

On Wednesday, October 17, 2012, at approximately 3:00 p.m., the Kentucky State Police Special Response Team executed the arrest warrants of Vernon and Debra Calloway. They were arrested without incident at their residence on Vine Hill Road outside of Hartford. Both Vernon Calloway and Debra Calloway were charged with one count of Murder; one count of Kidnapping; one count of Tampering with Physical Evidence and one count of Retaliation against a Participant in a Legal Process. All four charges are felonies. They were lodged in the Ohio County Detention Center in Hartford

KSP detectives presented this case to the Ohio County Grand Jury on Tuesday, October 16, 2012 after new information was discovered. The grand jury handed down an indictment warrant for Vernon and Debra Calloway. Vernon Calloway is the ex-brother-in-law to Patricia Calloway. Debra Calloway would be the ex-sister-in-law to Patricia Calloway. The Kentucky State Police have been investigating the suspicious disappearance of Patricia Calloway since March, 1993. She was last seen at her place of her employment in Hartford.

The investigating officer, Sergeant Bryan Whittaker should be given credit for solving this 19-

year-old murder mystery. Darrell Kessinger said he now hopes he can put this all behind him and start the real grieving process for his sister. He said, "It's like climbing a mountain. I haven't reached the summit yet, but I'm hoping we can now find her remains and get the opportunity to put her to rest."

Debra Calloway, Mug shot courtesy of Ohio County Police

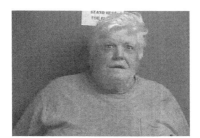

Vernon "Gene" Calloway
Mug shots courtesy of Ohio County Police

When Darrell Kessinger learned of the arrests, he called me immediately and told me, "You should see Gene's face in his mug shot!" He looks like he just saw a ghost." Darrell was truly elated that his sister may get justice after all these years. He was more hopeful than ever that he may get to properly bury his sister. It is obvious from the mug shot that Gene never expected to be caught. Debra's mug shot is smug, more than anything. I knew after looking at her mug shot, it wouldn't be the last Darrell heard from her. The next call I got from Darrell was not a happy one.

According to the KSP press release, the arrests were made in light of new evidence. What new evidence? We already know that Jimmy told police about seeing Patsy's body in the back of Gene's truck, very early on after she went missing with his brother. Did Mildred come out and admit that it was Debra she saw walking down highway 231? That's probably the case, but it doesn't explain why Gene wasn't arrested long ago. The detective and prosecutor who were in pursuit of justice now, had nothing to do with the debacle that occurred with KSP when Patsy first went missing. Detective Whittaker and Prosecutor Tim Coleman just had to put the pieces together. Also, in those days, it was much more difficult to get a conviction without a body. With family members now willing to testify, it was a much easier case to present to a jury. I suspect this is one reason why the arrests came about.

Once the pair was incarcerated, Debra made her attempt to exonerate herself from the situation. She called family members and told them that she saw Gene burying something in the back yard in a small box. She asked them to go dig up the items. They did as she requested, and when they located this box Debra screamed, "That's it! That's it!" If Debra didn't know what was in that box, why was she so elated? This question would be asked by the prosecutor at trial. The box contained a confession letter and a map to Patsy's remains as written out by Gene Calloway. We'll get to this topic later, but for now it will suffice to know that Gene Calloway admitted to killing Patsy in a confession letter. After that phone recording, police were able to obtain that confession letter. Larry Calloway has yet to be arrested for Conspiracy to Commit Murder, for Patsy Calloway.

Chapter Fifteen: Bonding Out

On May 3rd, 2013, just 6 ½ months after their arrest, I receive a phone call from Darrell Kessinger who was almost in tears. He told me that after their bond hearing, Debra got out of jail on a $30 filing fee and that Gene was being released too. He couldn't believe it. I know we're all innocent until proven guilty, but geez, the prosecutor had a witness to seeing Patsy's body and a confession letter. Why would the judge let them get out on bond? I'm still stunned!

Just after my call from Darrell, I confirmed that the report from him was in fact true. Darrell insisted that Gene wasn't sick, but was just faking again. I had heard stories from Larry's wife Shirley that Gene was great at faking illness and used that same technique with police before. Shirley said he'd once faked having mini-strokes to get out of jail. She said on one occasion, Gene was released from jail because he played sick, but as soon as he got out, he was seen out helping a friend rebuild a garage, lifting heavy objects and such. She said that while he was in jail, he told the jailer he was sick and pretended to faint and they took Gene to the hospital. A little while later, he was released from jail due to illness and stress.

I needed to follow up on their release, but I couldn't just print up something that wasn't verifiable so I asked Darrell, "Can you prove that Gene is faking?" Darrell said he was headed to KY to find out more. I told him, "If you can get any proof that I can use, send it." Off he headed back to Kentucky from Arkansas. Of course, my mind is blown that a judge would just let this confessed murderer walk free on house arrest. Was it because the confession letter hadn't been admitted into evidence yet? I can't answer that, but I knew they had it before the bond hearing, because Darrell had called and told me about it when the family member discovered the box.

When Darrell was in KY, he called me and told me he was pissed off because Gene was out riding his lawnmower. I told Darrell, "Get a picture!" He said he didn't have a camera phone. I told him, "Borrow one if you have to. Just get the damn picture!" "When you get it, email it to me immediately." It wasn't long after that, and Darrell called me and told me he got it. The following is a portion of my article on MissingPersonsNews that reflects what occurred:

"Originally the couple's bond was set at $500,000 each. After a bond hearing, Debra Calloway's bond was reduced to $10,000. By law, she was only required to pay 10% of that bond. Inmates are given a $100 per day reduction of bond for time served while awaiting trial. That reduced Debra Calloway's bond down to nothing owed after only 10 days. She was released to await trial at home on a $30 clerk filing fee. Vernon Calloway recently had a bond hearing and his bond was reduced to 10% of $50,000 cash or property or the $5,000 equivalent.

Photo courtesy of Darrell Kessinger

Darrell Kessinger (left) Larry Calloway (right)

According to sources, his bond was reduced due to illness and hardship. It is believed by some that Vernon Gene Calloway is nearly bed bound, and staying in jail to await trial would be too difficult for him to withstand. He was released from Ohio County Jail to house arrest on May 2nd, 2013 after posting the reduced bond. The above shown photo was taken just days ago and was provided by the victim's brother, Darrell Kessinger. Vernon Calloway is featured in the photo, while riding a lawnmower at his home. Because of HIPPA laws, it is impossible to obtain this man's medical records.

Since the release of Gene Calloway, Darrell Kessinger has headed up a small team of protestors in

Ohio County, to show their frustration in their local justice system in Hartford. They are protesting the release of Vernon Gene Calloway and his wife Debra Calloway, the accused murderers.

Darrell Kessinger stated that he is concerned with their release because aside from the murder and kidnapping charges, they were also charged with two other felonies, tampering with physical evidence, and intimidating a witness. Kessinger states that neighbors of Vernon and Debra Calloway are in fear for their lives knowing they have an accused murderer living near them. Kessinger says that in Kentucky, you can sit in jail for a year or two on a drug arrest, but if you're charged with murder, it's easier to get out of jail in Ohio County. He also states that the judge in the bond hearings missed an opportunity to bargain for his sister's remains. Her body has not been recovered. Kessinger states that the judge, if he was going to release him, should've demanded to know where Patsy's remains are located. He states that his sister's case has been blundered since the beginning of her disappearance and he fears that he will never see justice for Patsy Calloway.

When asked if he had any response from the prosecutor's office or from county officials regarding the release of Gene Calloway, Kessinger states that the local Sheriff, David Thompson, came down to the protest site and offered his support in what they're doing. Darrell said although he feels bad for them, Sheriff Thompson said it wouldn't do them much good to protest. Kessinger believes that Vernon Gene Calloway is a master at feigning illness and this is just another way of controlling those around him.

Kessinger and other supporters believe that the local public officials blundered again. Darrell Kessinger states, "It angers me that this man is out leisurely mowing his lawn and doing yard work, and I don't have my sister. I can't even bury her and they just let him go home to do yard work because he's too sick to be in jail? Where is the justice in that? My sister has been taken from us and this man gets to be at home while he awaits trial in the comfort of his own bed with all the comforts of his home.""

I posted this last article on May 14th, 2013 after I'd gotten that very distressed call from Darrell. It's unimaginable that someone using drugs will get a sentence of up to three years in the state of Kentucky for a single offense, yet a suspected murderer can bond out on just $5,000. Many drug offenders aren't able to post bond. Gene Calloway however, was out riding his lawn mower. He was a confessed murderer! Nothing anyone can say will ever rationalize this for me. What is wrong with the laws in our states and country? Why do they always seem to protect the criminals and not the victims? This was another epic failure on the part of our justice system. This man was charged with Capitol murder!

I told Darrell, I didn't feel there was any way Gene and Debra would tell them where Patsy's body was at that point, because that would mean they'd have to admit guilt under oath. They were charged with first degree murder and a plea agreement would have to be in the works in order for that to happen, because it was a death penalty case. I didn't see the prosecutor budging on that.

We know that after Gene and Debra's arrest, phone calls were recorded with Debra telling someone that she "saw Gene burying something in her back yard." When the family members went to the spot where Debra told them to dig, they found the box with a confession letter and map to Patsy's body. Now, how could she not know what was in that box? She directed them to go find it! Any idiot could see she knew exactly what was in there. In that confession letter, Gene admitted to killing Patsy. It's clear that Debra was attempting to exonerate herself, but Gene admitted to the killing. So why did they release him from jail on a mere $5,000 bond? I concur with Darrell in that they missed an opportunity to barter for Patsy's remains.

In response to the question of why he thinks they let him go, Darrell states, "Because they messed up again. They have the damn confession letter, so why did they let him out of jail without getting Patsy back? This is the kind of frustration I've been dealing with since Patsy first went missing," said Darrell. I told him, "It's not the same as the big city. When suspected murderers go behind bars, the prosecutors use every tool in their box to find out what happened. They had the tool box, but didn't know how to use the tools in it! These are small town cops who are not used to the day to day grind of dealing with murderers." It was all I could think of to offer up comfort at that moment. I had no real answer for his question. I still don't have that answer. That's a good question for KY officials as well. All those bleeding hearts out there who think we should consider the criminals rights, this could've been you in Darrell's shoes. What if it was your family member? How would you feel?

Chapter Sixteen: Hospice for a Killer

Two months after Gene's release from jail, on Thursday, July 11th, 2013, Vernon Eugene Calloway passed away in his home. He was awaiting trial for kidnapping and Capitol murder. However, he'd been released from jail on May 2nd, 2013 due to physical illness on $5,000 bond, even though he was facing charges that carried the death penalty. He was receiving hospice care in his home. At this point, it was my opinion he should've rotted away in jail. I can't see the justice in this. This man had people caring for him during his hour of need, while he had inflicted so much pain on the lives of others in the past.

The police and prosecutor had a confession letter, but the KY state budget didn't have the finances to care for this murderer, so they let him go home to die. Although there is a confession letter from Gene and a map to Patsy's remains, the family still hasn't been able to put her to rest. Darrell Kessinger assures me that he won't rest until he is able to bring Patsy home. For those who mourn the loss of Gene, I beg you to feel for Patsy and her family. All of this seems like a huge injustice that was served up to the family and then I remember, "You know where you came from and you know where you're going." People need to keep this in mind.

I've worked on over 300 missing and murdered victim's cases in one capacity or another. I've helped out a lot of law enforcement agencies even though they can't admit it for court reasons. Saying you're a psychic or remote viewer would be laughed away by any defense. People refuse to acknowledge what they cannot understand. But, I can see visuals of this much information about a murder case, which I did in Patsy's case and many others. When all I'm given is the victim's name and sometimes a photo, where does that information come from? Yes that's right. It comes from God. You can choose not to believe it, but that's ok. He has given me something to help out families that I can never thank him enough for. If he wants me to know it, he will reveal it. Knowing this and many other things he's shown me, I know that there is a heaven and a hell. I know that our Father in Heaven is our ultimate judge and jury. Even though Gene Calloway passed away before going to jail, I'm confident that he will face the ultimate judge, our heavenly Father. This is what puts my mind at ease.

You know, Gene died awaiting trial that possibly carried the death penalty. No way am I vain and I can't speak for the Lord our God. My guess is GOD thought he would take care of that so her family didn't have to suffer through watching him at trial. I'm sure the thought of his trial made Gene increasingly terrified of what was to come, because killing the weak is a most cowardly act. You rarely see a murderer go up against a worthy opponent. They go after the weak, because they are weak. It's ironic that so many people were afraid of Gene Calloway, but in the end, he was the one who was terrified. Trial or not, Gene knew his judgment was coming. I believe this is what ultimately caused his death before the trial. The fact remains that Gene got away with the murder of Patsy and perhaps others.

Although Vernon Gene Calloway passed away, Debra Calloway still had to face her day in court. After her release on $0 bond and a $30 filing fee, Debra was supposed to be on house arrest. At the protests of Patsy's family members, it was reported to me by Darrell and others that Debra showed up taunting and laughing at the protestors. She believed she'd never be caught and that the prosecution's case wouldn't stand up in court. It's even been reported that she got up in Darrell's face and laughed and said, "You can't prove nothing!" That's what Gene thought and well that's true, Darrell couldn't prove anything, but the prosecution could. He has the power of law and a prosecutor's mind. She's just a stupid criminal. After taunting the family during their protests with her smugness, I anxiously awaited to see her shock once she's convicted of her crimes.

Chapter Seventeen: The Trial Goes Forward

The case was presented in court by Prosecutor Tim Coleman like a master of the arts. One by one, the witnesses took the stand to tell of their part in the Patricia Kessinger Calloway disappearance. Larry Calloway spoke of how he paid his brother $1,000 to burn down the house belonging to him and Patsy on August 1st, 1991. He told the jury how he pled guilty to those charges in 1995, after the disappearance of his live-in ex-wife, but Vernon Gene was acquitted in 1996. Larry testified that he and Gene and Debra all planned the arson together. So why wouldn't they plan the murder together?

His sister Mildred spoke of how she pulled up along highway SR231 and saw Debra dressed up as Patsy. Darrell said Mildred was rambling on in court, pointing at Debbie and yelling, "You know it was you dressed up as Patsy down there. You know it was you!" The Prosecutor asked Mildred why she didn't come forward earlier. Mildred said, "Because he's my brother and I loved him."

Debra Calloway's son's ex-wife testified that she'd in fact saw the wig and a brown coat at Debbie and Gene's house. Jimmy Calloway testified that he was turning states evidence and that he saw Patsy's body in the back of Gene Calloway's truck. He also testified that later he'd seen Debra Calloway helping her common-law husband Gene, cleaning out the back of the truck. The carpets were ripped out and were saturated with Patsy's blood. According to him, there was dirt and grass on the undercarriage of the vehicle. He'd also seen the carpet from the truck in the trash cans at a later time.

How could Debra Calloway dispute all of this evidence when the prosecutor had a confession letter and a roughly drawn map to Patsy's body from Gene Calloway? Well in Gene's confession letter, he made an attempt at exonerating his wife Debra and his brother Larry. According to Darrell, the confession letter stated, "I killed Patsy. No one had nothing to do with it but me. Not Debbie, not Larry, not nobody." But his confession letter couldn't explain why Debra was dressed up in a wig, nurse's uniform, and trench coat. It couldn't explain to the jurors why she was seen cleaning out Gene's truck and disposing of evidence. It couldn't explain why she had a handful of family members that finally stood up to tell the truth against her. Debra Calloway would have to take the stand.

Visibly shaken, Debra made her way to the witness stand to testify in her own defense. It was the only option she had left. I'm contented to know that the prosecutor would make crushed ice out of this icy bitch who thought she was so much smarter than everyone else. Debra got on the stand and disputed that the purpose for wearing those items was to appear to be Patsy. She said that Gene made her dress up in the wig and trench coat when he forced her to have sex with other men. Debra denied ever wearing those items on the day Patsy Calloway disappeared. She maintained in court that she believes Patsy Calloway just walked away from her life. She also said that she believed her husband Vernon Gene killed Patsy. As a journalist, my question is, "which one is it?" Either you believe your husband killed her or you believe she walked away from her life, or you're lying." I believe the latter is correct.

Debra testified that Gene was a very jealous man. The prosecutor questioned her on this because she also said he forced her to dress up and have sex with other men. It didn't take the prosecutor long to wipe up the floor with Debbie's smugness and lies. He laid her lies bare in the courtroom for everybody to see. Her own brother-in-law testified that Debra was there when the arson deal went down. This also gave her motive to help in Patsy's murder. When prosecutor Tim Coleman finished with Debra Calloway, she didn't look like the smug, nasty woman who was capable of participating in and planning a murder. She looked old and defeated. But what would the jury think about this cold, calculating woman?

Debra's defense attorney tried to point the finger at everyone except Debra Calloway. He even tried to point the finger at Shirley's mother. He questioned Shirley about a fight that had taken place before Patsy went missing. He said, "Wasn't it your mother that beat up Patsy?" According to Darrell, Shirley's mom, Barbara Phelps and another woman Sharon Mattingly, beat Patsy to a pulp back in 1991. He said that Patsy showed up at his mom's house in Arkansas and their mother told them she was beat to a bloody pulp, after she confronted Shirley about her affair with Larry. I wondered why the defense attorney didn't put the squeeze on Larry Calloway. Then it occurred to me, if he did that, Debra would have to admit guilt, in order to have knowledge of it.

Chapter Eighteen: Finally, Some Justice for Patsy

She had no idea that it would be the last time anyone saw her. In a bizarre twist of what began as arson, Patsy's fate would be sealed as victim of a vicious and monstrous people, a victim of premeditated murder. Vernon Gene Calloway was acquitted of the arson charges in 1996. He died before he could be convicted of Patsy's murder. There are still some unanswered questions. What did they do to Patsy after she was in their control? They had to have a precise plan in place in order for them to carry this out so cryptically and precisely.

Gene used the newspaper article to lure Patsy away from her work. Was that marriage application staged for the newspaper to assist in the plot? If that's the case, again, Larry had to be involved in the planning. Gene knew of Patsy's infatuation with Larry and that this would upset her enough, so he could convince her to leave with him. Debbie needed to dress up as Patsy to make people believe Patsy was somewhere else, other than with Gene when she disappeared. With Patsy now under his thumb, he eventually murdered her. However Gene needed someone to blame it on and make it appear that he had nothing to do with it. Crime? What crime? In order to do that, he needed a scapegoat. Larry was the perfect scapegoat or co-conspirator. He was having an affair with a teenager he'd got pregnant for the 2nd time. They picked a day that was the one year anniversary of Patsy filing for divorce and Larry turning over the property to Patsy. It was a very calculated plan. They also needed an out, so that's why Debra dressed up in a trench coat, a nurse's uniform and a wig to make her look like Patsy. She was seen walking down the country road in Beaver Dam, KY, right after Patsy went missing. This was to make it look like Patsy was walking away from her life.

Prosecuting attorney Tim Coleman pointed out that Debra Calloway told several different versions of her accounts during testimony; of the day's events that unfolded. He proved to the court that Debra Calloway was a liar and helped plan Patsy's murder. Sgt. Bryan Whittaker testified that prior investigative work revealed that the carpet had been removed from Vernon Gene Calloway's truck, and the truck was thoroughly cleaned, coinciding with Jimmy Calloway's testimony.

Now everything would be in the hands of the jury. Would they see the whole truth, or would they let this calculating woman go?

**Image courtesy of Ohio
County Detention Center**

On August 6th, 2014, Debra Calloway was found guilty of the crimes of Facilitating Murder; Tampering with Physical Evidence; and Intimidation of a Participant in the Legal Process. As the verdict was read, she breathed a sigh of relief that she wasn't convicted for premeditated murder. However, fear washed over her when they read the other verdicts. Like Gene Calloway after his arrest, she looked like she'd just seen a ghost. Was it enough? I believe she should've spent the rest of her life in prison. Maybe she will. I believe she helped plan the murder. I also believe that the purpose of killing Patsy wasn't just for arson, but for sexual purposes. Debra testified that Gene made her wear the wig and have sex with other men. She also testified that her husband was an extremely jealous man who wouldn't let her out of his sight. Like I said before, criminals often mix lies with the truth. Would he be so jealous if she had sex with another woman? I suspect this isn't their first time perpetrating kidnapping and murder.

Gene Calloway was all about dominance and control. He tried to control everyone around him.

Birds of a feather flock together. From the first, I got the feeling that Patsy's case was like the Hooker case. That's what I told Darrell from the very beginning. I believe Gene Calloway and Debra Calloway were playing sex games. I believe that they both wanted Patsy Calloway sexually, not just Gene. He lured her out of her work and pretended to console her. He said they'd confront Larry, but their plan was far more evil. She was hurt, primed, and ready, and he knew it. I believe he showed her that newspaper to try and convince her that everyone was messing with everyone, including her beloved Larry. I believe that Patsy was sickened at the prospect of that and threatened Gene to call police.

Darrell believes that Gene told Patsy that Larry and Shirley were at her trailer at that very moment. Otherwise, Patsy wouldn't go with him unless he forced her using a weapon. I also know his intention was to kill her. Once Patsy was under Gene's control, she had no escape. Exactly what happened after Gene got Patsy into his control is somewhat of a mystery, until Jimmy Calloway saw her remains in the back of Gene's truck. If she went home to her trailer to find Larry and Shirley, that made it easy for him to attack her in her own home. Was Larry there when it happened? I can't answer that, but I suspect he got there not long after or was outside in the car with Debra. According to Darrell Kessinger, Vicki Hoheimer told him at her house one day that, Gene raped Patsy and Debra stood there and watched. Supposedly, Vicki didn't testify and claimed that she couldn't because her Multiple Sclerosis was causing her memory problems. I didn't see that in the visual flashes in my head. I saw what I saw and I suspect what I suspect. Gene admitted to killing Patsy, but Debra played a role in the facilitation of that killing and I believe more.

Hunter's trailer court is right in town. Patsy left her work at the nursing home at 10:30a.m. Jimmy testified seeing Patsy's body around noon that day. What happened during that time in-between? We know that Debra was dressed up like Patsy, but it wasn't until later that afternoon around 2:30 p.m., when Mildred reported seeing her walking down SR231. We know Patsy's car was moved, but we don't know when it was moved.

Maryanne left the nursing home right after Patsy did to go alert Larry and Shirley. It doesn't make sense that he wouldn't go past Gene and Debra's trailer which was right there in town. I'm not buying it. He was already told that Patsy left her work with Gene by Maryanne. Why didn't he go directly to Gene's house? Or did he? Did he see something going on at Gene and Debra's trailer that he didn't report to police or was he at his own trailer during the murder? Was he in on it? Was Shirley Calloway there? Did Gene threaten him at the trailer? At this point, the trial had concluded, but it left so many unanswered questions about what Larry actually did that day. Who really moved her car? I'm wondering if Larry Calloway had a life insurance policy on Patsy. Was Larry out for revenge?

The judge gave Mrs. Calloway the opportunity to apologize or make a statement to the family of the victim, to which she abstained from speaking. Prosecutor Coleman demanded a harsh sentencing due to her lack of remorse. The jury recommended a sentence of 11 years in total which is the maximum sentences for the crimes she was convicted of. I'm certain if they would've given her more time if they could've. Darrell said he was thrilled when she left the courtroom in handcuffs. He finally felt vindicated for the taunts he endured during this and felt "some" justice for his sister.

After the trial concluded, I spoke with Darrell. He said that he and Patsy's family are happy about the convictions. He said, "I'm happy, relieved, and exhausted. I just need to take a break for a bit. It's been 21 years that I've been trying to get justice for my sister and I need to let it all settle in." Darrell said he spoke to one of the Calloway sisters and asked her why she didn't come forward before. He said she replied that she just wanted to protect her brother, same as she did in court. I'm sickened by the thought of that. She should be jailed for obstruction of justice. I asked Darrell about the recovery of his sister's remains. He said, "Well, a lot was brought out in court about her being buried up on Andy Anderson's farm. I don't know if they can get a warrant or not. We'll see what happens, but that's the last promise I made to my sister... to bring her home."

Darrell goes on to say that this case was never unsolved, but unproven. He said he knew in his heart in 1993 that Gene Calloway killed his sister, but was conflicted if Larry had anything to do with it or not. After many years of fact gathering, he knew what Gene and Debra had done to Patsy. Some of that time was going over speech analysis and remote viewing with me. The police just needed to get the cooperation of the family in order to get convictions. Without their testimony, the law had no case.

In the rolling hills of Kentucky, it's often like that. Back in the hollers, nobody speaks of such things, because the countryside is far and wide. Their blood runs thick and deep, even if it means covering up a murder. It savage reality to see a family such as the Callaway's. On one hand, they're welded to each other like the sap on a pine cone. However, if there's a chance they can turn states evidence to get a lighter sentence for a crime they've committed, they turn on each other like pit vipers.

Before the discovery of the confession letter and map and other papers, Darrell received a mysterious call to meet at a car wash in Beaver Dam. Darrell called me and told me that this mysterious person wanted to meet him. I'd advised him not to go when he told me this, because they wouldn't reveal who they were or what they knew. Darrell reassured me that he would be wearing his weapon.

He left Arkansas and headed back to Kentucky. He found the car was in Beaver Dam. When he spoke to the man on the phone, he was told to pull his car in between the concrete barriers and stay behind the wall. He did as he was told. He stood there and was told not to come around the wall. Darrell could've been killed right there at the carwash. Darrell said he couldn't recognize the voice, but the man told him that he knew Gene had killed Patsy. Darrell said he told the man, "I already knew that." The mysterious man said, "Larry knew about it because Gene had come to him the very next day and Gene told Larry not to worry about it, that it's been taken care of." Darrell was also told by the man, "I'm a friend and don't be afraid." The man told him to be careful because his life could be in danger. Darrell told the man that all he wanted was to bring his sister home and that he'd never stop. With that, the man left. He was never identified. I pray God above that this man finds the courage to come forward. Gene is gone. What is he so afraid of?

There is still that lingering question. According to statement analysis, Larry did know of the murder plot, but that isn't always full-proof. In our interview, he told a whole bushel of lies which are obvious to a deaf man. He warned Patsy about Gene, but what exactly did he say to her? Why would he warn Patsy about anything? Did he see Gene do these things in the past?

Darrell told me that during this investigation he and Detective Whittaker had words more than once. He said he can understand how the police need to work, but he is retired military. In the military, you only have one choice and that is to do your job. Darrell said the two have very different personalities, but the same goal. He hopes that in the near future, they can work together to find Patsy's remains. He said a lot of credit should be given to Detective Bryan Whittaker and Prosecuting Attorney Tim Coleman for helping to resolve the now 21-year-old case of his sister.

One of the officers told me "off –the-record," that he believes Darrell Kessinger is "certifiable and crazy." This officer, who shall remain nameless, has told me that same thing about Darrell on more than one occasion. To this hard working man, I say, "How would you feel?" You've got a murderer right there in your face and his accomplice, taunting you and laughing at you and telling you, "you'll never get justice." Mr. Kessinger is a trained, retired, military veteran who's served in Desert Storm and other military operations. They could've been terminated with extreme prejudice and Darrell could've gotten away with it like Gene did. Instead, he chose not only to pursue justice for his sister, but to help others in their desperate time of need. Darrell Kessinger is a God fearing man and an inspiration to many. While some may think it's crazy to pursue his sister's case that long and to go toe to toe with his sister's killers, Darrell Kessinger is no coward. I'm proud to call him my friend. Crazy or not, I could only hope that someone would love me as much as he loves Patsy.

On September 4th, 2014, Debra Calloway was sentenced to 12 years in prison for her crimes. She was taken to the Kentucky Correctional Institute for Women in Pee Wee Valley, KY. The judge added another year to what the jury recommended because Debra committed perjury in court, according to Darrell Kessinger. She is to serve the 12 full years consecutively with no chance of parole. She will be 72-years-old when her sentence is finished.

Chapter Nineteen: Collateral Damage

It's hard to imagine what a family goes through when a loved one is murdered or missing. God knows the thoughts that run through a person's mind. For those people, I pray every day that they can find some sort of peace. So for them, I will offer them something. Back in the beginning when I first met Darrell, I told him I felt like Larry Calloway was a pedophile and sexual predator, but not a murderer, although I wasn't certain if he helped plan Patsy's murder or not.

On August 5th, 2014, Detectives Bryan Whittaker and Matt Wise charged 65-year-old Larry Ray Calloway with two counts of 1st Degree Sexual Assault, with both victims being under 12-years-old. Matt Wise was the arresting officer. The alleged incidents occurred in 1991 and 2001.

On September 4th, 2014, Larry Calloway, while still incarcerated, was served more warrants because charges were added. The charges include Nine(9) counts of Sexual Abuse 1st degree, victim under 12-years-old; One (1) count of incest, victim under 12-years-old; One (1) count of Rape 1st degree, victim under 12-years-old; and Two (2) counts of Sodomy, victim under 12-years-old.

I receive this information from the KSP PAO Trooper Corey King. He reports, "The investigation was initiated by the Kentucky State Police when four female victims reported allegations on Calloway. It was alleged that around 1977 – 2005, Calloway had inappropriate sexual relations with the victims who were all under 12 years old. Detective Matt Wise served the indictment warrants on Calloway who was already being held in the Ohio County Detention Center in Hartford on a $100,000 full cash bond. This investigation is ongoing. Any other victims or anyone with information regarding Larry Calloway are encouraged to contact Detective Matt Wise at the Kentucky State Police Post 16 – Henderson at 270.826.3312 or 800.222.5555.

It was a very smart move for the officers to wait until his testimony was finished in Debra's murder trial, before law enforcement officials arrested Larry Calloway. He is currently awaiting trial at the Ohio County Detention Center. He may not be charged with the murder of Patsy Calloway, but he'll still probably serve out the rest of his life in prison. At almost 66-years-old, that won't be an easy sentence for him.

Larry Calloway, Mug shot courtesy of Ohio County Detention Center

As a journalist, I report things that are presented to me. I record and verify as much information as possible. As a remote viewer or intuitive, I try to write it all down and verify when possible. Part of my interview with Larry Calloway, which was recorded, included details about his relations with his wife Shirley. I asked Larry about his relationship with Shirley because I had that image in my head about him that I couldn't let go of. Sometimes but not always, victims of pedophilia become the perpetrator. This is what I feel for Larry Calloway as a remote viewer and intuitive. The following statements reflect part of my interview with Larry Calloway that was left out of the article:

Cummins: "I can see where it makes you look bad, because you're her husband and you're having an affair with a young girl."

Calloway: "Exactly."

Cummins: "And she was underage and so forth."

Calloway: "No no no no"

Cummins: "Well, she was 17, when she had your first son."

Calloway: "Well, I'm not, a young girl turned my head. It happens. It happens every day."

Cummins: "Well, you guys are married now. You've got four kids. I was just confirming what Darrell had told me, because I don't want to print anything that's a lie, or anything that I can't verify. Do you understand?

Calloway: "Exactly."

This was an excerpt of the interview with Larry. I moved away from that line of questioning in the beginning, because I knew Larry would be afraid he would get into trouble. I later followed up:

Cummins: "Okay, so you were living with your ex-wife and you were living with your girlfriend at the same time?"

Calloway: "No no. I wasn't living with the girlfriend."

Cummins: "Oh, but you said you were in Shirley's apartment, so you were just kind of staying there?"

Calloway: "It was her apartment."

Cummins: "Oh, it was Shirley's apartment. It wasn't your apartment?"

Calloway: "Exactly."

Cummins: So this 16-year-old girl had an apartment by herself?"

Calloway: "No. She wasn't 16. That's what I'm trying to tell you."

Cummins: "Oh. They've got her birthday. They've got her as 39-years-old now. Is this correct?"

Calloway: "Yeah, she's 39."

Cummins: "So she was 16."

Calloway: "No. No. Uh Uh. She couldn't have been."

Cummins: "Yeah hon. She was 16, because she had your oldest son in 1990. I've got the report, not that that matters."

Calloway: "I mean, that matters to me cause it don't add up. She moved out from my mom and dad's when she was 18."

Cummins: "She must not have been telling you the truth about her birthday. She was 16 when you got her pregnant and almost 17 when she had the baby."

Calloway: "I'll have to go back and check that with you. It don't add up for me.

Well, Larry said he may have to go back and check, but I'm sure he knew at the time he got her pregnant that Shirley was only 16-years-old. Larry Ray Calloway was born on October, 16th, 1948. Shirley Marie Calloway was born in July, 1973. Shirley was 17 when she gave birth to their oldest son and 16 when he got her pregnant. Larry was 42-years-old at the time his son was born. He is 24 years and 9 months older than his current wife Shirley. Shirley was just a child when they started having a sexual relationship.

I find it interesting that when Larry speaks of his affair with now current wife Shirley, he says, "Well, I'm not, a young girl turned my head. It happens. It happens every day."

Yes Larry, I guess it does happen every day with you. Not anymore. You claimed that you weren't messing with a child and you also claimed you had nothing to do with Patsy's murder. I'm not buying it. Gene attempted to exonerate Debra and Larry in his confession letter. We already know that all of them lied. If Larry had nothing to do with Patsy's murder, why would Gene even mention it? He mentioned Debra and we know she's guilty. It's reasonable to deduce that Larry helped plan it. Of course, I don't have proof of that, except for the taped recording of our interview where he says that he can "confirm" Gene had Patsy's keys.

After our first long interview, Larry and Shirley Calloway called me back and asked me to take this portion of the interview and leave it out of the article. He was afraid he would get into trouble for messing with a young girl, and also for personal reasons. I didn't want to cover up for what he was doing, but at the time, I had to put Patsy's case above other possible crimes. So for that purpose, I took it out of my article. I told him, "That was back in the late 1980s and early 90s." You're married to her and have four children together. Nobody is going to care about that particular thing almost 20 years later. They're worried about Patsy's murder and what role you played in it, if any, and finding her and bringing her home."

Notice that Larry said, "It don't add up." Well if Larry had $40 in his pocket and spent $26, he'd know he had $14 dollars left! It is my understanding that Larry started seeing Shirley long before he got her pregnant. He's not fooling anyone and he didn't at the time. Any grown person knows he was taking advantage of a child who wasn't fully mature in her decision making. Consent or not, Larry knew that.

I'm not defending Larry Calloway when I say this, but I believe he was once a victim, and then became the perpetrator. This is what I feel for him as an intuitive. His interview revealed that Shirley was a young teen when they started having sexual relations. I don't know that Larry being abused is a fact. It's just a feeling I have. He's not been convicted of anything and is still awaiting trial. But people are coming out of the woodwork claiming sexual abuses by him and members of his family. According to Darrell Kessinger, he and his sister, along with three of Larry Calloway's own children have been sexually assaulted by Larry or one of the Calloway brothers. We don't know how many others are out there, but I pray they have the courage to come forward. "Please, come out of the shadow of fear! Let justice prevail and let the healing being." His actions are NOT your fault!

On September 1st, 2014, I spoke with Patsy and Larry's daughter Tanya in an interview. According to Tanya, Shirley is only one year older than her. She said that her dad would take her camping as a young child. She said that when she was 11 or 12 years old, Shirley would always accompany them. She said that on several occasions, she was pretending to be asleep, but she was awake. She said her father Larry and then 12 or 13-year-old Shirley, were having sex in the tent right next to her. She said she'd lie still under the covers and keep her eyes closed and pretend to sleep, but she knew full well what was going on. She said she'd seen them making out on other occasions.

On Thursday, September 3rd, 2014, I spoke with Ruby Renee, Shirley and Larry's second oldest child. She told me that her father in fact, molested her and she is one of the girls who has reported it to police. She said many of her family members have turned their back on her for pressing charges. Another child of Larry's said the same thing. Renee said, "I have no desire to go back to Kentucky except for the trial." She said she no longer has a mother, because her mother is defending Larry. She went on to say that she wants to get a college degree and pursue a career in law enforcement. She said she wants to protect other people from what she and others have endured and she's going to stand on her own two feet to do it. I wish these young women all the luck in the world and the love of GOD to shelter them and guide them in their endeavors.

Who knows what goes on in the farms and back woods of Kentucky? Well I'll tell you if you don't know. God knows. I was only given Patsy's name to begin with. I was able to fill in most of the gaps for Darrell. God showed me only what I needed to see, to help this suffering man, Darrell Kessinger. Without God, that isn't possible. Don't ever doubt his power. He sees all and reigns over all of us. He gave me a gift to use and I have worked hundreds of cases because of what he's given me and others. It's not the judgment in this world that we should concern ourselves with, but the next. So, to all of these perpetrators of violence, know that GOD is watching and you will reap what you sew. So many people have suffered at the hands of the Calloway brothers and Debra Calloway. But I'm confident that they will all have their judgment day, even if it's not in court. As an intuitive, it's not possible to prevent the crimes, but that doesn't mean there aren't witnesses to it, by the grace of God.

As far as Darrell is concerned, well that is another chapter. Recently he reported to me that two of the Calloway brothers attempted several times, to sexually assault him, as a young boy. It took Darrell over 55 years to admit it happened to him. One of the men has passed away, the other is still out there. To this man, you know who you are, God is watching. If you want to heal, you need to admit it; acknowledge what you've done wrong; accept the consequences; repent; and try to make amends.

Now, I didn't come here to preach to my readers, you can take what I say as fact, or you can leave it. If you want to verify it, I put some of my reading on Psychiccrimefighter.com, which is time-dated September 26th, 2012. Just look up Patricia Ann Kessinger Calloway, Psychiccrimefighter.com on the internet. You'll see part of my reading. I didn't post all of it because it was personal to the family and very graphic. It is what it is.

As far as my feeling goes that Gene Calloway was a serial killer, aside from what I've already shown you in this novel, information has come to me from a reliable source. It has been reported to me that some paperwork was found that had to do with Gene Calloway and a missing girl was mentioned. A name was written on a piece of paper, Heather Teague. Teague went missing several years after Patsy's murder. She was similar height and stature of Patsy.

There are those out there who believe the police already knew who her abductor was, but like Patsy, her body has never been found. The man police originally suspected committed suicide prior to them arresting him. I believe that man had ill intentions, but I don't believe he is responsible for Heather's disappearance, but another woman who lived somewhere in the Carolina's. I don't pick up on anything for that man in regard to Heather. I'm wondering if her remains are also down on that farm near Patsy. Who were the other victims of Gene? The Kentucky State Police have conducted searches recently in the past 2 months for Heather. We may never know what happened for sure, but God does. Officer Corey King, POA, KSP reports the following:

(Henderson, KY) August 26th will mark the 19th anniversary of the kidnapping of Heather D. Teague. According to KSP, Teague was last seen on August 26, 1995 at Newburgh Beach in Henderson County.

Victim: Heather D. Teague
White female, 23 years of age at the time of the kidnapping.

Location: Newburgh Beach, Henderson (Henderson County), Kentucky.

Last Seen: 19 years ago.

A witness observed the victim being kidnapped at gunpoint from Newburgh Beach in Henderson County.

Multiple KSP detectives have worked diligently on this case and have exhausted many leads; however, no arrests have been made nor has Teague been located. The Kentucky State Police is committed to providing answers for the Teague family and has made many proactive attempts to garner newer leads.

Detectives have recently sought information that led them to excavate two core areas. Various retention basins used in a livestock operation near John Steele

Road (Henderson County) were recently drained. Its contents were dug out and spread across a field. Nothing of evidentiary value was found.

A 20 foot deep cistern (in an undisclosed area) was also identified by KSP detectives as a potential concern. A submersible camera was used to view the contents of the contained well. Unsatisfied, detectives then excavated the entire cistern and inspected its contents. Both endeavors provided no evidence to this case.

Furthermore, as social media has become more mainstream for many people, KSP detectives continually monitor networking sites such as Topix, Face Book, Twitter and other similar chat sites.

We respectfully request if anyone has any information regarding this case and/or the kidnapping of Heather Teague, please contact KSP Post 16 at 270.826.3312 or text an anonymous tip to KSP at: 67283, KSPTIP ("your message").

Photo courtesy of Kentucky State Police

What the officer doesn't mention is that a witness saw Teague being taken from the beach area. Her abductor was described as wearing a wig.

Chapter Twenty: Searching for Patsy

As Darrell had mentioned, a lot was brought up in court about Patsy's remains being at Andy Anderson's farm. Gene Calloway drew a rough map to where he buried Patsy on the property. The property is a farm with many mature trees. It's a heavily wooded area with a carpet of leaves and brush. Darrell had asked Andy Anderson for permission to search the property, prior to the reveal of this information in court. He said at first, Andy agreed to allow the teams to search. Then he changed his mind. Darrell was very angry about this. Again, the police weren't searching for Patsy. Mr. Anderson, according to Darrell refused. But then, Patsy's son, Shane, spoke with Mr. Anderson and asked him if they could come out and search for his mother.

According to Darrell, he'd once again agreed for them to search the property, he just didn't want a bunch of people there without law enforcement involvement. That's a reasonable request because he didn't want his property torn up unnecessarily, not that they would. After all, these are professional search and rescue teams. They wanted to be able to bring in their cadaver dogs to see if they'd get a hit on the property. It's also been reported by Darrell that Gene Calloway's son worked for Any Anderson for many years. I don't know if this played a role in his decision not to allow them to search, but Darrell believes it has. According to Mr. Kessinger, Mr. Anderson owns the local media in that area. He said that his sister had only a couple of very small articles written about her disappearance. He said that he believes that's why it was never reported in the paper when Patsy went missing. One can only hope that's not the situation.

After the trial of Debra Calloway and prior to her sentencing, Shane Calloway, Patsy's son, snuck onto the property of Andy Anderson. He went to the farm, to see if he could find the spot that Gene Calloway indicated on the map where he buried Patsy. I got a call from Darrell Kessinger about his nephew. He said that Shane called him crying hysterically. He told me that Shane found the spot where he believed his mother was buried. He found a tree that had a cross cut into it, and a bone, which may or may not have been human. I told him to call his nephew back and tell him to stop what he was doing and immediately call police. I didn't want to see Patsy's son get into trouble for being out there on the property. I told Darrell to hang up from me and call the police. Darrell said he first tried to get in touch with Detective Whittaker and left him a message on his phone. He said that Detective Whittaker hadn't answered so that's when he called me. I again told Darrell to call his nephew back and tell him to stop digging and wait for police. He told me that Shane said, "I'm not going to let my mom spend another night on this property. She's coming home tonight." I could hear the anguish in his words. Darrell told me that he was going to call him back and call the police.

When I hung up the phone with Darrell, I called Kentucky State Police in Ohio County and left a message for Detective Whittaker. He called me back and I told him what Patsy's son had found. I explained to him that he was still out on the property and was waiting for him. Detective Whittaker asked me, "Why would Darrell call you instead of me?" I didn't want to state the obvious to him. He told me he was going to check it out. Other officers had already been dispatched to the scene. Detective Whittaker said, "What is it that he thinks he's found out there?" I said, "According to Darrell, he's found a bone. He's also found a tree with a cross cut into it." With that, the officer said he was on the way.

Photo courtesy of Darrell Kessinger

Not long after I spoke with Detective Whittaker, Darrell called me back and asked me why I called the police. I told him, "If that bone is human, maybe they'll search the property now. If it is where your sister's remains are located, I don't want them to use that Patsy's own son suspiciously found her remains, at Debra's trial. Her lawyer could try to say that he knew where his mother was buried all along. I didn't want to see Shane be the one to find his mother and I didn't want him to get shot while trespassing. Nor did I want to see him get in trouble with the police for disturbing a crime scene or interfering with an investigation."

Darrell had sent me the pictures that Shane had sent to them. He asked me if I thought it was a human bone or not. I told him I couldn't tell from the pictures, but it appeared to be part of a scapula. I couldn't tell if it was human or animal and that's what I relayed to him. Darrell said that Shane also found some other items at the same site. He told me he found two RC Cola bottles dating back to 1993. He said that Shane had found an empty plastic bottle of motor oil.

Photo courtesy of Darrell Kessinger

How awful to think that Patsy's own son would be the one to find her remains. Darrell told me that he was on his way back to Kentucky. I told him to call me back as soon as he knew what was going on.

Over the next few days, Darrell and I kept in contact over the phone. Darrell said his nephew Shane told him that when Detective Whittaker showed up, he asked Shane the same question that he asked me, "What is it you think you've found?" Darrell said they took the soda bottles and empty oil bottle. He said they told Shane that they would come back out and search the next week.

When Darrell got there for the search, he said that the area wasn't taped off or anything. He told me that they'd dug in a few spots, where they found tree stumps, which is what Gene had indicated on his map. He said they had a small back hoe out there. When it started raining, they told them that they were going to "pack it in." Darrell said they dug in three or four spots, maybe two feet down. He said it was ridiculous. They didn't find any more bones, so they called off the search. He told me that they haven't been back out there since.

I asked Darrell if he spoke to Detective Whittaker about it. He said, "Bryan Whittaker told me that they're not going to tear up this man's property looking for my sister." Darrell told me that the coroner was out there and said that the bone was an animal bone and it wasn't human. Since then, the trial of Debra Calloway has been completed. She was taken off to prison, but we're no closer to recovering Patsy's remains. There has to be cooperation in order to do that.

I called my friend Shellee Hale back and asked her, what the chances were that they'd find Patsy's skeletal remains out there and what they would have to do. Shellee said that sometimes, they'll take a cadaver dog to the site. She said they'll use hollow rods and hammer them down into the ground. She said that sometimes, this will release gases that were trapped beneath the soil, and the dogs may be able to pick up on a scent. After 21 years, the chances are not likely that they'll find her, unless they have a good idea of where he buried her. She said they're more likely to find her clothing and purse   if they were buried with her.

With that empty bottle of motor oil sitting there, I have to wonder if Gene used it to dispose of her remains. Did he burn her body after they murdered her? Darrell believes they already had a hole dug for Patsy. He sent me information about the weather during that time and said that the ground was still not thawed at the time she went missing. He said there were a few warm days prior to her disappearance. It is a good possibility that the grave was dug ahead of time. After all, they plotted out the murder so viciously and precisely that it took the police over 21 years to solve it and get a conviction.

How can anyone get peace out of this, knowing she's still out there somewhere. If he burned her, there is the chance they will never find anything. They'll never know if they don't search. My question is, "What is the harm in bringing in cadaver dogs?" That's not the same as "tearing up a man's property." I realize it's been over 21 years and the percentage odds are small that they'll get a hit, but there is still a chance. In the military, it is the rule that no one is left behind. That doesn't seem to be the case back home. That makes it even more difficult for Darrell Kessinger. He was off fighting for our country while his own sister was being brutally murdered and left behind.

Recently, I got images and flashes in my mind, of Gene Calloway as an old man. He's standing in a rain poncho and jeans at the foot of that tree. The rain is cold and coming down hard, but he is burning, like fire through his veins. He is bare-footed. He drops down to his knees and is digging at the dirt with his fingers. The dirt falls through his fingers like flour through a sifter. There are tears streaming down his face and a look of terror in his eyes. He is like a dog, digging in the dirt for what was once there. He tries to rip off the rain poncho to no avail. In my mind, he is condemned to face the fires of hell until Patsy is found. If Patsy isn't found, he will burn eternally. His spirit is there. He is tortured, desperately wishing he could undo what he has done. Now his haunted soul searches for answers. There is nothing he can do from the other side, except watch. His fate lies at the mercy of God. He has been bound by what he left for this world, which sealed up his fate. He's not only being punished for what he's done to Patsy, but for what he has done to her family and those who loved her as well. He is being punished for the good of life that he's stolen away from this world. As Theresa, Patsy's sister, put it long ago, "It's in God's hands now." In my mind, our supreme ruler has made his judgment. I am saddened to see this in my mind, but God's judgment is righteous.

Not every story has a happy ending. Some of them are the most horrific. Patsy has been missing for well over 21 years. Her brother Darrell had bought her a burial plot with a marker. The searches have halted and the grave site is still empty. How sad for Patsy and her family. When I ask God about Patsy's welfare, all I see in my mind's eyes now, are prisms of light. I feel like she is at peace in heaven.

Chapter Twenty-One: Patsy's Legacy - The Untold Story

Patsy Calloway was a very giving mother and woman who worked as a nursing assistant because she cared about people. She loved her job and wanted nothing more than to raise her children and serve the American dream. She was raised in the hills of Kentucky by her father and with her younger brother Darrell. With the absence of his own mother from the home, Patsy was her stand-in. Darrell and his sister's relationship was very tightly bonded. As a child she was his protector.

Darrell and I had met because of his search for his sister. During his quest to find Patsy, he began going to meetings to find out what he needed to do in his quest. He went to a candlelight vigil in remembrance of Jodi Powers. That's where he met her mother, Belinda Powers. This was long before he and I made phone contact. At one of those meetings he spoke with Belinda Powers, the founder of the Jodi Powers Search and Rescue Technologies or JPRST. The two became fast friends and Kessinger joined the search and rescue team. But the back story behind JPRST is one of tragedy.

Jodi Powers was reported missing on August 30th, 2010, by her mother, Belinda Powers. A month after Jodi was reported missing her body was located near a power line not far from her home. The coroner stated that there was no sign of trauma, but there were indications of foul play as reported by the police. To date, no one has been charged in her disappearance or death of Jody Powers. While Patsy's case has been somewhat resolved, Jody's is somewhat of a mystery to police.

The beauty of Darrell and Belinda's coming together is one of humble humanity and kindness shown in both of them. They have overcome unsurmountable odds to turn tragedy into hope for many others. I believe it is by the grace of God that these two people became friends. They have continued to work on many searches together over the past four years and will continue in the future. Not only are they friends, but in my eyes, family, bonded by what many people can't have the depth to understand.

When I asked Darrell initially if I could write their story, he was hesitant. He said people had accused him of trying to get book deals and movie deals. Darrell was angry that people thought he wanted to make a profit from his sister's horrific murder. Because of that, he wanted some of the proceeds from this novel to go to the JPRST. He said he doesn't want to make any money off of his sister's tragic death and refuses to accept any. Darrell has spent over $50,000 dollars out of his own pocket while searching for his sister and pursuing justice for Patsy. He said it's what any loving brother would do. "If Patsy were alive, I know in my heart she'd do it for me." He also said he'd like for some of the proceeds to go to MissingPersonsNews. Shellee Hale and I have spent thousands of dollars on countless cases as victim's advocates and search and rescue workers out of our own pockets. Darrell said that he wants his sister's legacy to be one of hope and caring for others, because that's what she tried to do while she was alive. In honor of his wishes and as part of the JPRST; MissingPersonsNews; and Psychiccrimefighter; I'd like to ask you to join in.

If you'd like to be a part of a search and rescue/recovery team, please contact your local search and rescue agency. Over 2800 people go missing in the US daily, and some of those people are never recovered. Search and Rescue teams can always use volunteers. If you don't want to join a team, I ask that you please just walk your own property. Take a friend on a hike and go search the woods of your local park. Many people are right in the public when they are discovered. If you prefer, you can also make a contribution to the Jodi Powers Search and Rescue Technologies at JPRST.org, or send your donation to:

JPRST, P.O. Box 121
Madisonville, KY, 42431

Or you can contribute to Psychiccrimefighter or MissingPersonsNews by making a donation at Camandago.com. Although Patsy hasn't been recovered yet, her legacy will be one of hope for the families of those out there who are still missing. May their cries be heard and their prayers answered. **Patsy**, you will **NEVER** be forgotten.

By Tina M. Cummins, Victim's Advocate